VR~VIRTUAL REALITY

FROM EARLY ILLUSIONS TO A WORLD YOU CAN STEP INTO

SERIES "IN TWELVE EVENINGS

BOOK 7

VITA HARWOOD

WHAT DO I ALREADY KNOW ABOUT THIS?

TEST YOUR KNOWLEDGE!

~12 LESSONS ~TESTS ~EXPERIMENTS ~ANSWERS ~VOCABULARY

~FURTHER READING~ THEHAPPYSTORYGARDEN

CONTENTS

Course Program 1
Introduction 5
Lesson 1. Can You Trick the Brain into Believing in Another World? 9
Lesson 2. Who First Tried to Build a Machine That Could Create Another Reality? 25
Lesson 3. How Do Two Tiny Screens Turn into a Vast Space? 39
Lesson 4. How Does the Headset Know How You Are Moving? 53
Lesson 5. Why Can Virtual Reality Make You Feel Sick? 67
Lesson 6. What Is a Virtual World Made Of? 81
Lesson 7. Why Isn't a Beautiful Virtual World Enough? 95
Lesson 8. Who Are You Inside a Virtual World? 109
Lesson 9. Why Do Surgeons, Pilots, and Engineers Need Worlds That Do Not Exist? 123
Lesson 10. Can You Learn What a Classroom Cannot Show You? 137
Lesson 11. What Does Virtual Reality Know About You? 151
Lesson 12. What Happens If Virtual Worlds Become as Ordinary as Screens? 165
Afterword 181
Answers to the Tests 185
General Glossary 195
Resources 201
What to Read and Watch Next 207

Welcome to TheHappyStoryGarden! 209

COURSE PROGRAM

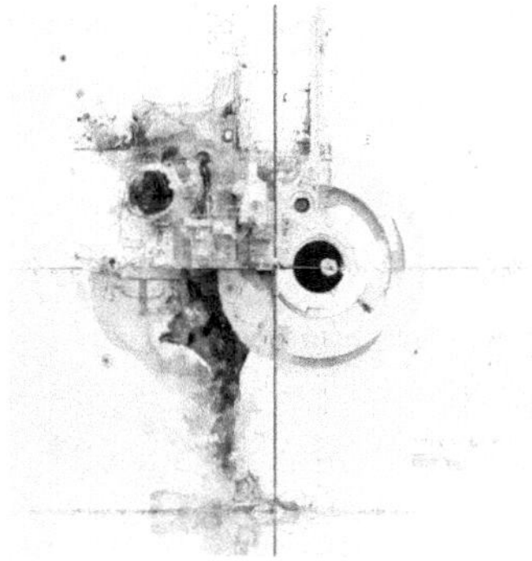

Over twelve evenings, we will move from VR's central illusion to its consequences. First we will ask why a digital scene can feel like a place, then work through optics, tracking, and cybersickness before entering the developer's workshop. The final lessons turn to real-world uses of VR, learning, data, and the future of spatial interfaces.

BLOCK I. HOW DID WE GET THE IDEA OF STEPPING INSIDE AN IMAGE?

Lesson 1. Can You Trick the Brain into Believing in Another World?

Lesson 2. Who First Tried to Build a Machine That Could Create Another Reality?

BLOCK II. HOW DO YOU SHOW THE BRAIN A WORLD THAT IS NOT THERE?

Lesson 3. How Do Two Tiny Screens Turn into a Vast Space?

Lesson 4. How Does the Headset Know How You Are Moving?

Lesson 5. Why Can Virtual Reality Make You Feel Sick?

BLOCK III. HOW DO YOU BUILD A WORLD YOU CAN STEP INTO?

Lesson 6. What Is a Virtual World Made Of?

Lesson 7. Why Isn't a Beautiful Virtual World Enough?

Lesson 8. Who Are You Inside a Virtual World?

BLOCK IV. WHAT HAPPENS WHEN VR LEAVES THE GAME ROOM?

Lesson 9. Why Do Surgeons, Pilots, and Engineers Need Worlds That Do Not Exist?

Lesson 10. Can You Learn What a Classroom Cannot Show You?

BLOCK V. WHEN VIRTUAL REALITY BECOMES PART OF REAL LIFE

Lesson 11. What Does Virtual Reality Know About You?

Lesson 12. What Happens If Virtual Worlds Become as Ordinary as Screens?

AT THE END OF THE BOOK

Answers to all 120 test questions, with explanations; a general glossary; resources for each lesson; and a section called "What to Read and Watch Next."

RECURRING FEATURES IN EVERY LESSON

Main text; "Portrait"; "Plot Twist"; key terms; a ten-question test; and a home experiment. The course-long assignment is called "My Virtual World": from lesson to lesson, you will build the concept for a VR project of your own.

INTRODUCTION

Virtual reality begins with a simple contradiction. You may know perfectly well that you are standing on the floor of your own room and still step back from the edge of a virtual rooftop. The computer has not moved you anywhere. It has only arranged vision, sound, and movement so that, for a moment, your body takes a digital scene seriously.

That contradiction is exactly what makes VR interesting. This is not one technology and not one entertainment genre. Optics, computer graphics, motion sensors, perception psychology, interaction design, medicine, education, and privacy all meet here. To understand VR, it is not enough to list the parts of a headset. We need to follow the entire loop: what the system measures, what it shows a person, how that person responds, and what the computer does with the response.

The course is built as an investigation. In the first two lessons, we will separate virtual reality from film, screen-based games, and augmented reality, then see how separate inventions gradually came together into a modern system. Lessons 3, 4, and 5 cover vision, motion tracking, and cybersickness. Here it will become clear why even a beautiful scene fails if it lags behind your head or disagrees with your vestibular system.

The next three evenings are devoted to building a virtual world. We will see how geometry becomes a surface, how an engine calculates light and collisions, why a menu designed for a monitor cannot simply be transplanted into VR, and why an avatar needs to match the movement of the body. These lessons make one point especially clear: a VR developer is not designing a picture, but the behavior of a system around a person.

In Lessons 9 and 10, VR leaves the game room. We will look at simulators, medical and therapeutic uses, design, and education. One strict rule applies here: an impressive demonstration is not proof of benefit. If someone claims that VR teaches a skill or helps a patient, we need to ask what was measured, what it was compared with, and whether the effect transfers to a real task.

The last two evenings are about data and the future. A headset measures the position of your head and hands, and some systems also track gaze and facial movement. That can produce a far denser stream of behavioral data than an ordinary web page typically receives. At the same time, the boundary between VR, AR, and MR is becoming less rigid. The future of this field may look less like a separate "virtual world" and more like a set of spatial interfaces that appear around us when we need them.

This book is not trying to convince you that VR will inevitably change everything. Nor is it trying to prove that VR will remain a niche toy. We will distinguish what already works from what exists as a prototype and what is still a promise. That skill is more useful than any list of current headset models: devices change quickly, while good questions about technology age much more slowly.

HOW THE COURSE WORKS

Each lesson is designed for one evening and ends with a test. The answers are collected at the back of the book so that the test can first do its job as a check on your reasoning. After the test comes a home experiment that requires no special laboratory and, in most cases, no VR headset either.

The course-long assignment, "My Virtual World," requires no programming. In Lesson 1, you will decide why your project exists. Then you will define what the user sees, how they move, what they interact with, what kind of avatar they have, what data the system needs, and what safety rules should apply. By the twelfth evening, you will have a VR application concept that can be discussed as a project rather than a fantasy.

ABOUT THE TECHNOLOGY AND THE MATH

This course is written for readers aged 15 and up with an ordinary school-level background. Formulas appear only when the physical meaning would otherwise be lost. Advanced optics, computer graphics, and tracking algorithms certainly exist, but here we will examine causes and relationships rather than university-level mathematics.

ABOUT HEALTH AND MEDICAL USES

The sections on cybersickness, therapy, and rehabilitation explain scientific and engineering principles; they do not provide medical advice. People respond to VR differently, and clinical uses are evaluated for particular conditions and protocols. Significant discomfort during a VR session should not be endured in the hope of "getting used to it."

LESSON 1. CAN YOU TRICK THE BRAIN INTO BELIEVING IN ANOTHER WORLD?

THE ROOM IS STILL THE ROOM

Imagine that you are standing on a level floor. You are wearing a headset and holding controllers. In front of you is a virtual plank suspended between the roofs of skyscrapers. You know there is carpet under your feet. Yet your body may still tense up, and stepping toward the drawn edge can feel deeply unpleasant. Virtual reality begins in that contradiction.

VR does not transport the body to another place. It changes the stream of information the brain uses to judge where the body is and what surrounds it. Vision reports one environment, sound supports it, and every turn of the head immediately changes the view. When those signals agree well enough, presence can emerge: the person experiences the digital space as the place they are in right now.

That does not mean the user forgets the room. They understand that they are looking at a computer-generated scene. But perception and behavior begin to follow some of that scene's rules. A virtual height can therefore be frightening, a flying object can make you duck, and an avatar that comes too close can invade your sense of personal space.

WHY A SCREEN STILL FEELS LIKE A SCREEN

A film can absorb your attention, and a game on a monitor can make you care intensely about what happens. But an ordinary screen preserves a boundary: the image is in front of you. In VR, the display moves with your head and fills a large part of your field of view. The computer recalculates the scene from your new viewpoint.

Lean toward a virtual table and it should come closer. Look around a column and you should see the part that was hidden. The user stops being a spectator with a fixed camera and gains a position inside the scene.

That is why it is more useful to think of VR as a perception-and-action loop: you move, the system measures the movement, changes the image and sound, you perceive the response, and you act again.

IMMERSION AND PRESENCE

Immersion usually describes technical properties of the system: how much of your vision it covers, how accurately it tracks you, whether sound is spatial, and how your hands are controlled. Presence describes the user's experience: how strongly they feel that they are in the virtual place.

The two are related, but they are not the same. A technically excellent headset does not guarantee presence if the scene behaves implausibly. Conversely, simple graphics can be convincing if the world responds consistently to what you do. The brain cares not only about detail, but about whether the signals agree.

VR, AR, MR, AND XR

VR usually replaces the visible environment with a digital one. Augmented reality, or AR, leaves the physical world in view and adds digital elements. Mixed reality, or MR, emphasizes a close relationship between digital objects, the geometry of the room, and real objects. XR is used as an umbrella term for this family of technologies.

The boundaries between these terms shift, so a more useful set of questions is: how much of reality does the system replace, how much does it preserve, and how closely are digital objects tied to the user's movement and the physical space?

WHY BUILD ARTIFICIAL WORLDS?

Entertainment is only one answer. An artificial environment can repeat a dangerous situation safely, change scale, reveal invisible processes, and simulate something that would be difficult, expensive, or impossible to reproduce physically.

A pilot can train without a real aircraft. A student can examine anatomy in three dimensions. An architect can walk through a building before it is built. A psychotherapist can present frightening situations under controlled conditions. A scientist can alter experimental conditions with a precision that is difficult to achieve in the real world.

But the more convincing a virtual environment becomes, the more serious the question of influence becomes. If a digital event produces a real reaction, should we dismiss it as "just a picture"? We will return to that question in Lessons 11 and 12.

WHY IS THE BRAIN WILLING TO ACCEPT AN ARTIFICIAL ENVIRONMENT AT ALL?

Human perception does not work like a video camera passively recording everything around it. The brain continually assembles a picture of the world from incomplete signals and checks that picture against its own predictions. We do not consciously calculate every distance or compare every shadow with a physics handbook. The perceptual system looks for the most plausible explanation of what the eyes, ears, skin, muscles, and vestibular system are reporting together. That is why virtual reality can feel convincing even when the user knows it is artificial. Knowledge and perception operate at different speeds and solve different problems.

The link between action and response matters especially. In the real world, turning your head immediately changes what you see and hear. If a digital environment does the same thing quickly and consistently enough, the brain receives a familiar pattern. A wall stays put when you look elsewhere. A sound source keeps its direction. A virtual table gets closer when you lean toward it. This stability contributes to what researchers call the place illusion: the feeling that space really surrounds you even though you understand that it is digital.

Presence has another side. Something can happen in a virtual scene that a person knows is impossible or staged, yet the body may still react. VR research sometimes distinguishes the sense of being in a place from the plausibility of events. The first asks, "Do I feel that I am here?" The second asks, "Do events behave as if they are really happening to me?" Realistic graphics do not always help. It often matters more that a character looks where they should, an object responds predictably to touch, and a sound matches the position of its source.

This is why virtual reality cannot be defined by a single device. A headset alone does not create a complete experience. If it merely shows ordinary flat video with no relationship to the user's movements, some of VR's central properties disappear. On the other hand, a research system may look technically modest and still create strong presence through accurate tracking and a well-designed interactive scene. VR is a system: display, optics, sensors, rendering, sound, controls, and human perception have to work together.

It is also useful to separate presence from emotional engagement. A reader can lose track of time in a novel, a player can become deeply invested in a game on a monitor, and a film viewer can flinch. That is engagement, but it is not necessarily spatial presence. VR adds another layer: the user does not only follow an event, but experiences their own position relative to objects. This is especially obvious in actions involving the body. A virtual object can make someone step back because it violates their preferred distance. A height can make them cautious because moving forward is perceived as moving their own body toward an edge.

This brings us to the first serious qualification in the course. The phrase "VR tricks the brain" is convenient as a title, but too crude as a scientific explanation. The brain does not switch off critical thought or stop knowing about the headset. A more accurate description is that the system provides sensory signals consistent enough with the rules of natural perception that some orientation and behavioral mechanisms respond to the digital environment as surrounding space. It is less dramatic, but more precise.

That view will matter later. When we discuss cybersickness, we will see that the problem also arises from relationships among signals. When we reach avatars, we will see that the brain can incorporate digital hands into its current model of the body. And in the lesson on privacy, we will see that convincing spatial interaction can require much richer behavioral data than an ordinary website typically collects. The central tension of VR is visible already in Lesson 1: the better the system understands your movements and responses, the more convincing it can become, and the more responsibly that information must be handled.

There is another useful way to think about virtual reality: as a system of hypotheses. The brain is continually estimating where objects are and what will happen after a movement. Turn your head to the right and you expect a stationary door to shift leftward in your field of view. Raise your hand and you expect its position to change accordingly. VR becomes convincing when it confirms such expectations quickly and without obvious contradictions.

This explains why small errors can sometimes be more destructive than obvious stylization. A cartoon-like scene can be internally consistent and therefore feel stable. An almost photorealistic scene with wrong shadows, a lagging character, or an object that passes through your hand can suddenly advertise its artificiality. Visual realism and believable behavior are not the same thing.

Strong presence also does not require the user to forget the surrounding world. A person can understand that they are in a laboratory and still behave cautiously near a virtual edge. This double awareness matters throughout the ethics of VR. We cannot excuse an unpleasant or manipulative experience by saying, "it isn't real," when the user's reaction is real.

That is why researchers measure not only subjective reports such as "how strongly did you feel that you were there?" but also behavior: distance from a virtual character, movement speed, protective reactions, and errors while performing a task. Combining methods helps clarify what presence means in a particular experiment.

For a developer, presence is not a button that can be switched on. It is supported by accurate tracking, low latency, coherent sound, understandable interactions, believable scale, and the absence of unexpected contradictions. Each coming lesson will examine one of these components. By the end of the course, we will return to our opening question and see that "believing in another world" is not one illusion but the coordinated work of many systems.

There is an important difference between a system that merely puts a screen in front of your eyes and one that constructs a stable space. If the image does not change when your head moves, you quickly feel that you are looking at a picture attached to your face. When objects keep their positions relative to the virtual world, an external space begins to emerge. Tracking, then, is not a technical extra added to VR. It is one of the mechanisms of presence itself.

Presence also depends on the task. People notice spatial inconsistencies more strongly when they have to do something: reach, walk around an obstacle, or catch an object. Passive viewing can hide errors that action reveals instantly. This suggests a developer's test: examine the environment not only with the eyes, but with the body. Where do you expect a surface to be? How far away is an object? Does the sound match its direction? Does the user understand the consequence of a movement?

This active component is what separates VR from many earlier technologies of illusion. A panorama surrounds you, a stereoscope creates depth, and cinema directs attention, but modern VR combines space with measured action. Its effect on a person therefore cannot be reduced to image quality. It is a computed environment that observes movement and responds to it. That response is the central subject of this course.

A simple thought experiment makes the point. Imagine a virtual room that looks convincing, but every turn of your head arrives late, the table shifts slightly, and the sound seems glued to the headphones. Technically, you are still looking at 3D graphics in a headset, but the sense of place quickly falls apart. Presence is not produced by one spectacular effect. It grows from the agreement among many small responses.

The brain is especially sensitive to broken causality. If you reach out and an object is grabbed before contact, if a door opens without an action, or if a character answers before you have finished speaking, the environment feels less reliable. In an ordinary game, such an error may be funny. In VR, it touches the user's sense of their own bodily position and therefore calls attention more strongly to the technical intermediary.

At the same time, a virtual world does not have to copy physics literally. It can let you fly, change scale, or teleport. An experience can remain convincing if the unusual rule is stable and understandable. The brain can accept a fantastical law if the system applies it consistently. This is one of VR's important freedoms: presence can coexist with the impossible.

That is why the word "reality" in the name does not mean a copy of our world. It refers to an experienced environment that responds consistently enough for a person to form expectations within it. Later we will see how medical, educational, and artistic applications use that freedom in different ways.

Lesson 1 gives us a useful test of mature VR: the user understands where they are, what they can do, and how the system will respond. If any one of those links keeps breaking, the headset remains an expensive screen. If all three work, even a stylized digital world can feel like a place.

PORTRAIT: MEL SLATER

British researcher Mel Slater has spent decades studying presence and human behavior in virtual environments. His work helped clarify the distinction between immersion, which describes properties of a system, and presence, the user's experience of being in a virtual place. He is especially known for research on virtual embodiment and social situations. A user can know an event is artificial and still respond as though it were happening nearby.

PLOT TWIST: A VIRTUAL DROP CAN TRIGGER THE BODY BEFORE DELIBERATE THOUGHT

A person may refuse to step off a virtual ledge while physically standing on a safe floor. This does not prove that the brain has been "completely fooled." Fast perceptual and motor-control systems can respond to visual threat before calm deliberation catches up.

KEY TERMS

Virtual reality (VR) – an interactive computer-generated environment that replaces the perceived surroundings with digital space.

Immersion – technical properties of a system that increase sensory coverage and strengthen the link to the user's actions.

Presence – the experience of being located inside a virtual space.

Interactivity – the ability of a system to respond to a user's actions.

AR – augmented reality, which adds digital elements to the physical world.

MR – mixed reality, in which digital objects are closely tied to physical space.

XR – an umbrella term for VR, AR, MR, and related technologies.

TEST

Choose one correct answer.

1. What most clearly distinguishes VR from a film?

a) High resolution

b) The system changes the scene in response to the user's movements

c) Controllers are required

d) Three-dimensional graphics

2. What does presence mean?

a) The experience of being in a virtual environment

b) The number of sensors

c) The quality of a model

d) The connection method

3. What best describes immersion?

a) Emotions alone

b) Story alone

c) The technical conditions that support immersion

d) The length of a session

4. What does AR do?

a) Completely hides the real world

b) Works only with sound

c) Always requires a closed headset

d) Adds digital elements to the physical world

. . .

5. Why can a virtual height be frightening?

a) The user always forgets about the room

b) Visual information can trigger a real protective response

c) The headset changes air pressure

d) The controller causes fear

6. What does interactivity mean?

a) The graphics are photorealistic

b) The user watches a video

c) The system is connected to the internet

d) The system responds to the user's actions

7. Which is the umbrella term?

a) XR

b) HMD

c) FPS

d) FOV

8. Why is photorealism not enough?

a) The brain cannot see realism

b) Realism is prohibited in VR

c) The environment must respond coherently to the user's actions

d) Presence depends only on sound

9. How does a VR user differ from a spectator?

a) The user is always standing

b) The user cannot hear the outside world

c) The user always sees their hands

d) The user changes the viewpoint through their own movements

10. Why use VR outside entertainment?

a) Only for advertising

b) To simulate difficult or dangerous situations safely

c) To replace every real-world activity

d) To eliminate the teacher

HOME EXPERIMENT

- Close one eye and hold up a finger. Alternate your focus between the finger and an object behind it, then open both eyes. Write down which cues help you judge distance. Begin the course-long project "My Virtual

World": imagine a place that would be worth entering virtually, and explain in one sentence why it exists.

- *In the next lesson, we will see why the road to VR began long before digital headsets, and why an old stereoscope was solving one of the same problems as a modern headset.*

~

LESSON 2. WHO FIRST TRIED TO BUILD A MACHINE THAT COULD CREATE ANOTHER REALITY?

BEFORE THE COMPUTER CAME THE STEREOSCOPE

The idea of showing a person a space that is not physically in front of them is older than the computer. In the nineteenth century, stereoscopes used two images of the same scene taken from slightly different viewpoints. Each eye saw a different picture, and the visual system combined them into a sense of depth.

For the history of VR, this matters as more than a museum curiosity. It is evidence that virtuality begins with perception.

Technology learned to give the eyes signals similar to those they receive from a three-dimensional world.

PANORAMAS AND THE DESIRE TO BE INSIDE THE PICTURE

Panoramic images surrounded the viewer and removed the familiar frame of a painting. A person stood at the center of the scene and could turn to look around it.

A panorama was not interactive, but it tackled a future VR problem: how to occupy the field of view and weaken the sense that one is looking at a flat image. The history of immersive technology was assembled from separate solutions: depth, visual coverage, movement, and interaction.

SENSORAMA: WHEN THE SCREEN WAS NO LONGER ENOUGH FOR CINEMA

In the mid-twentieth century, Morton Heilig worked on multisensory cinema. His Sensorama presented stereoscopic images, played sound, and added airflow and smells. It was not modern interactive VR: the computer did not recalculate the scene when the viewer turned their head. But the goal is recognizable, to address several senses at once and strengthen the feeling of presence.

Sensorama breaks the convenient legend of a single "inventor of VR." The technology grew out of cinema, optics, simulators, computer graphics, sensors, and research on perception.

SUTHERLAND'S HEADSET AND THE TURN OF THE HEAD

In 1968, Ivan Sutherland and Bob Sproull created one of the early computer systems with a head-mounted display. The apparatus was so heavy that its structure had to be suspended from the ceiling. It was later often nicknamed the Sword of Damocles.

Its importance was not comfort. The computer-generated image changed with the observer's head position. A central loop of future VR had appeared: movement is measured, the computer recalculates the scene, and the eyes receive a new view of the world.

WHY THE FIRST WAVES OF VR RECEDED

By the late twentieth century, VR had been declared an imminent revolution more than once. But a mass-market device needed many things at the same time: a fast computer, a lightweight display, accurate sensors, low latency, convenient controls, and an acceptable price.

If even one link was weak, the illusion broke down or the device became impractical. That is why the history of VR came in waves. Interest returned whenever displays, graphics processors, and sensors made another leap.

WHY MODERN VR FINALLY WORKED

In the 2010s, several mature technologies came together in one device. Small displays improved, inertial sensors became smaller and cheaper, graphics processors learned to draw complex scenes quickly, and position-tracking systems became practical for consumer hardware.

Sometimes a good idea waits for decades not because nobody understands the problem, but because the necessary components are still too large, too slow, or too expensive.

WHY THE HISTORY OF VR IS SEVERAL HISTORIES AT ONCE

Try to find a single birthday for virtual reality and you quickly run into a problem. Too many technologies solved different parts of the future task independently. Optics learned to create stereoscopic depth. Panoramas worked on surrounding the field of view. Flight simulators developed the idea of safe simulation. Computer graphics learned to build images from mathematical models. Sensors linked the image to head movement. Only their gradual combination made what we now call VR possible.

The nineteenth-century stereoscope is especially revealing. It did not create an interactive world, but it already exploited the physiology of binocular vision. A viewer saw two flat images and experienced depth. Stereoscopic photographs soon became a popular form of entertainment and a way to "visit" distant places without leaving home. This was not yet virtual reality in the modern sense, but an important cultural dream was already present: technology could create a feeling of access to a space that was not nearby.

Panoramas solved a different problem. Their makers tried to remove the ordinary frame of a picture and surround the viewer with an image. In some panorama buildings, the architecture deliberately concealed the boundaries of the canvas and helped sustain the illusion of a continuous scene. Here we can see an early principle of immersive design: sometimes credibility comes not from adding detail, but from removing signs of mediation. The less the viewer notices a frame, an edge of a screen, or a device, the easier it becomes to perceive an image as an environment.

In the twentieth century, the idea of a multisensory experience was added to vision. Morton Heilig thought of cinema as a medium that could work with more than image and sound. Sensorama was mechanically complicated and never became a mass-market product, but it looks strikingly familiar today: stereoscopic imagery, sound, airflow, and additional sensations were meant to strengthen presence. It is important not to turn Heilig into a prophet who somehow built modern VR in advance. His apparatus lacked the central interactivity of today's systems. But he clearly saw the problem of extending a medium beyond the flat screen.

Sutherland's work made the next fundamental step. The computer no longer merely displayed a prerecorded scene. It calculated the image according to the observer's position. That means the world exists as a model, while the view of it is constructed again and again. This logic distinguishes an interactive 3D environment from a film. If the user moves, the system does not search for a prepared frame; it calculates a new perspective. Modern engines apply the same idea on an incomparably more complex scale.

By the 1980s and 1990s, companies, laboratories, and art projects were explicitly talking about virtual reality. Data gloves, early HMDs, and CAVE systems, in which images were projected onto the walls of a room, appeared. Media interest was enormous. The technical constraints, however, remained severe: low resolution, heavy headsets, expensive computation, latency, and limited access to equipment. The public image of the technology developed faster than its everyday practicality.

The later success of consumer VR therefore cannot be explained by one brilliant idea. Smartphones helped mature small displays and inertial sensors, graphics processors became much more powerful, tracking algorithms improved, and component manufacturing became cheaper. What once required a laboratory could now fit into a comparatively compact device. The story resembles the development of many complex technologies: a mass-market breakthrough occurs when several curves of technological maturity cross at the same time.

This history is also a useful defense against technological prophecy. In different decades, VR was repeatedly declared a revolution that was almost here. Sometimes the forecasts were simply too early; sometimes the future took a different form. That is why, in the final lesson, we will not try to guess the date of a "complete metaverse." It is more reliable to ask which specific technical limits have already been removed, which remain, and what those changes actually mean for the user.

Another important branch of the story runs through simulators. A pilot benefits from learning not from an abstract picture of an aircraft, but in an environment where instruments, the view outside, and the aircraft's responses are linked to the pilot's actions. Early flight simulators were not VR in today's sense, but they established an important idea: a computationally or mechanically simulated environment can be valuable precisely because it allows a situation to be repeated safely.

Computer graphics added the ability to change the world in real time. Before interactive graphics, a panorama or stereoscopic photograph had to be prepared in advance. Afterward, the scene became computable. The user could receive a new view not because an artist had drawn thousands of frames beforehand, but because the computer knew the geometry of the objects.

Later, CAVE systems offered another route to immersion: images were projected onto walls around a person, sometimes with head tracking. This is a reminder that VR does not have to mean a headset. The central principle is an interactive spatial environment; the display itself can be built in different ways.

Consumer experiments of the 1990s show the danger of promising too much too early. The public understood the idea, but displays, computation, and tracking were not yet good enough to make the experience cheap, lightweight, and convincing at the same time. Disappointment did not mean the underlying principle was wrong. It meant the set of components had not reached the necessary maturity.

When small displays and inertial sensors were developed at mass scale for smartphones in the twenty-first century, VR unexpectedly benefited from another industry. This is a common path for technology: a crucial component is often improved for reasons unrelated to the product that will later use it. The history of VR is therefore also a history of technologies migrating between industries.

Instead of asking "Who invented VR?" it is more useful to ask "What problem did each stage solve?" The stereoscope gave depth, the panorama gave visual coverage, the simulator gave safe repetition, computer graphics gave a computable scene, and tracking linked the scene to movement. This view replaces a heroic legend with an engineering history.

The history of VR reveals another pattern: the boundaries among scientific instrument, simulator, entertainment system, and artistic medium have constantly been crossed. Tracking technologies developed for military or industrial work could later enter games. Graphics methods from entertainment were later used by architects and researchers. Dividing the story into separate "worlds" is therefore too simple.

The word virtual has shifted in meaning as well. In computer culture, it has long described something that exists in effect or function even though it is not a physical object in the ordinary sense. The phrase virtual reality succeeded partly because of this paradox: the environment is not physically present before the person, yet it produces real sensory and behavioral consequences.

By the end of the twentieth century, the public imagination often ran ahead of the technology. Books and films depicted complete digital immersion while real devices struggled with heavy optics and crude graphics. That gap still matters today. Science fiction can help formulate a dream, but engineering advances through specific constraints. The next lessons will take those constraints apart one by one.

Military research also mattered because difficult training tasks could justify expensive systems long before a mass market could. Simulators made it possible to study control and perception in conditions where a real mistake would be too costly. Over time, many principles developed for specialized tasks became increasingly available to civilian applications.

At the same time, artists and media researchers used immersive environments not for precise simulation, but for new forms of storytelling. This broadened the question: a virtual environment can do more than copy reality. It can create experiences that are impossible in the physical world. A user can enter an abstract visualization, inhabit a different scale, or move through invented architecture.

The rise of the term VR helped unite these scattered lines into one cultural image. But a shared label can hide important differences. A simulator is judged by skill transfer, an artwork by expression, and a game by the quality of interaction. The technological foundation may be similar, but the criteria for success differ.

The history also shows that components do not mature in sync. A good display is useless without tracking. Accurate tracking does little good if computation is too slow. A cheap headset will not become widespread without content that justifies buying it. A technological ecosystem requires hardware, software, and worthwhile tasks to mature together.

Modern VR is therefore not the final point in the story. It is simply the latest configuration of ideas that have been developing for a long time. In the next lessons, we will treat it not as a finished invention, but as a system in which old optical principles are joined to modern sensors and computation.

PORTRAIT: IVAN SUTHERLAND (1938–)

Ivan Sutherland entered the history of computer graphics before VR existed as a field. His Sketchpad work in the early 1960s showed that people could interact with a computer graphically. He later formulated the idea of an "ultimate display" in which a computer controls the objects a person perceives. The early HMD of 1968 was far from that ideal, but it established a direction: the image should depend on the observer's position.

PLOT TWIST: THE TERM "VIRTUAL REALITY" IS YOUNGER THAN THE IDEA

Precursors of VR appeared long before the expression virtual reality came into widespread use. The name took hold only after the core principles had already been developing for decades in different laboratories and industries.

KEY TERMS

Stereoscope – an optical device that presents a separate image to each eye.

Panorama – an image or environment that surrounds the viewer and extends the field of view.

Head-mounted display (HMD) – a display worn on the head.

Head tracking – measurement of head orientation and position so that the virtual camera can be updated.

Simulator – a system that reproduces the essential conditions of a real process.

Stereoscopy – the creation of a sense of depth by presenting different images to the two eyes.

Latency – the time between a user's action and the system's response.

TEST

Choose one correct answer.

1. Which principle of the stereoscope matters for VR?

a) A computer is required

b) A separate image is shown to each eye

c) Hand tracking

d) Spatial audio

2. What did panoramas provide?

a) Haptic feedback

b) Gesture recognition

c) Full interactivity

d) Wide visual coverage

3. How did Sensorama differ from ordinary cinema?

a) It used several sensory channels

b) It created networked VR

c) It always tracked the viewer's head

d) It ran on a game engine

4. Why was Sutherland's HMD important?

a) It was the first mass-market headset

b) It linked a computer-generated image to head position

c) It worked without a computer

d) It was the first to use smells

5. Why was the apparatus suspended from above?

a) For sound

b) For radio reception

c) Because it was very heavy

d) To hide the floor

6. Why is there no single inventor of VR?

a) No historical sources survive

b) The first devices were only toys

c) VR appeared only after the internet

d) The technology grew out of many different fields

7. What held back early mass-market VR?

a) Several essential components were still immature

b) There was no interest in 3D

c) HMDs were prohibited

d) It was impossible to show two images

8. What changed in the 2010s?

a) Sensors disappeared

b) Displays, computation, and tracking matured

c) VR abandoned graphics

d) Headsets became devices for film only

9. What does the history of VR show?

a) A good idea always reaches the mass market quickly

b) The name of a technology always comes first

c) An idea may have to wait for the right components

d) All inventions happen at the same time

10. Which question leads into Lesson 3?

a) How does the internet work?

b) Why do people like games?

c) How does a battery work?

d) How do the eyes derive depth from two images?

HOME EXPERIMENT

- Take two photographs of the same object from slightly different viewpoints. Compare which parts of the scene shift relative to the background. In your "My Virtual World" project, decide what kind of space surrounds the user: a room, a street, a laboratory, or an open landscape. Also choose the point where the user first appears.
- *In Lesson 3, we will examine VR's central optical trick: why two flat images can create a sense of depth and scale.*

LESSON 3. HOW DO TWO TINY SCREENS TURN INTO A VAST SPACE?

TWO EYES DO NOT SEE THE SAME THING

Look at a nearby object, first closing your left eye and then your right. The object seems to shift against the background. Your eyes occupy different points in space, so each retina receives a slightly different projection of the world. The brain uses that difference as one cue to depth.

VR uses the same principle: the system calculates two images of the same scene from slightly different viewpoints corresponding to the left and right eyes. Optics deliver each image to the appropriate eye. The visual system combines them, and flat displays become an experienced three-dimensional space.

DEPTH DOES NOT DEPEND ON A SINGLE CUE

Stereoscopy matters, but it is not the only cue. Perspective, occlusion, light, shadows, familiar size, and movement all help us judge distance. Motion parallax is especially useful: when the head moves, nearby objects shift across the field of view more than distant ones.

VR therefore has to do more than present a good stereo pair. It must keep updating that pair so that all depth cues remain consistent with the user's movement.

LENSES BETWEEN THE EYE AND THE SCREEN

A headset display is too close to the eyes to be viewed like a phone. Lenses create a virtual image at a more comfortable optical distance and make a larger portion of the display usable. The optics also introduce distortion, so the software pre-corrects the image before it reaches the eye.

The choice of lens affects headset size, sharpness, field of view, and the range of eye positions that work well. The simple act of "putting on a headset" hides a system of optical compromises.

FIELD OF VIEW AND THE FEELING OF A FRAME

Field of view, or FOV, describes the angular extent visible through the device. A narrow field of view feels more like looking through a window. A wider one can strengthen the sense of visual coverage, but it demands good optics and additional computation.

Human vision is not equally detailed across the whole field. We resolve fine detail much better in the center than in the periphery. Modern systems can therefore devote more computing power to the region where the user is actually looking.

THE STRANGE CONFLICT OF FOCUS

In the real world, when an object comes closer, the eyes both converge more strongly on it and change focus. In most VR displays, stereoscopic depth changes while the physical focusing distance remains almost constant. This is called the vergence-accommodation conflict.

It does not make VR impossible, but it is a reminder that a headset reproduces only some of the visual signals of the real world. We still do not have a complete copy of natural vision.

HOW A VIRTUAL CAMERA REPLACES A PHYSICAL VIEWPOINT

In ordinary 3D graphics, a camera is a mathematical viewpoint from which an image of the scene is constructed. In VR there are effectively two virtual cameras, one for the left eye and one for the right. They are separated by a small distance corresponding to the user's eye positions. If the geometry is correct, every surface occupies a slightly different place in the two images, giving the brain binocular disparity.

But depth in virtual reality does not come from one number. Imagine a long corridor. Even with one eye closed, you can tell that the walls converge in perspective, distant doors look smaller, and nearby objects block more distant ones. Move your head and the relative positions of objects change. These are monocular and dynamic depth cues. Good VR keeps them consistent with stereoscopic information. If one cue says an object is close while another behaves as though it were far away, the scene begins to feel strange.

Scale is also the result of agreement among cues. A virtual cup feels cup-sized not because the display shows it in "real centimeters," but because the brain judges it relative to hands, a table, perspective, and familiar objects. Scale errors are particularly obvious in VR because the user can move closer. An architectural scene that looked convincing on a monitor can suddenly resemble a dollhouse in a headset. The body detects the mismatch.

Headset optics make the problem harder. The flat display sits close to the eyes, but a lens changes the path of light so that the image is perceived at a more comfortable optical distance. Modern designs use different types of lenses, each with trade-offs in thickness, weight, brightness, sharpness, and visual artifacts. A specification such as "display resolution" therefore tells you very little by itself about how sharp the image will look to a particular user.

There is also individual fit. The distance between pupils varies from person to person. If the virtual cameras or optics do not align well with the actual eye positions, the image can become less comfortable and less natural. Devices therefore use mechanical or software adjustment for interpupillary distance, while more advanced systems may track the eyes. Once again, VR cannot be separated from the body: the geometry of the image must fit the geometry of the individual observer.

The vergence-accommodation conflict reveals a limit of current displays. In real life, when you shift your gaze from a distant wall to a pencil held close to your nose, your eyes both converge and refocus. In a typical VR headset, a virtual pencil may be stereoscopically close, yet the light still comes from the display through optics at an almost unchanged focal distance. The brain receives an unusual combination of signals. Most users can work with it, but it remains an engineering problem, especially in long sessions and for objects placed very close to the eyes.

One direction in display research involves variable focus and more complex light-field approaches. The goal is to provide the eye with more of the natural optical cues to depth. This is difficult: the device still has to remain light, fast, and bright enough. The future of VR displays therefore depends not on a single parameter such as "more pixels," but on optics, eye tracking, computation, and ergonomics advancing together.

Peripheral vision matters too. We see fine detail poorly at the edges of the visual field, but the periphery is very sensitive to motion and helps maintain orientation. A wide field of view can therefore strengthen presence, yet it also makes motion errors more noticeable and can increase discomfort. This becomes especially important in Lesson 5: a signal that helps you feel inside a scene can work against you when it conflicts with other sensory information.

Virtual depth also depends on familiar size. If an ordinary door stands in front of you, you already have a rough expectation of its scale. If a digital door is twice as tall as expected, the whole scene may begin to feel different. Developers therefore check the world against the human body, not only against numbers in a 3D editor.

Very close objects create particular difficulties. On a monitor, an interface can be placed only a few virtual centimeters from the camera and cause no obvious problem. In a headset, the same element may demand strong eye convergence and become uncomfortable. Spatial interfaces are therefore usually kept at a comfortable distance and avoid prolonged reading on planes placed too close to the user.

Image sharpness is uneven as well. Optics may have a region in which the image is especially clear, while quality falls toward the edges. Users instinctively move their eyes, and sometimes their whole head, to inspect a detail. Optical ergonomics therefore influence behavior and fatigue as well as image quality.

Eye tracking makes it possible to respond dynamically to where the user is looking. Foveated rendering takes advantage of the fact that central vision is much more detailed than peripheral vision. The system can save resources in areas where the eye could not resolve fine detail anyway. It is an elegant engineering move: a limitation of human vision becomes a way to improve performance.

Eye tracking, however, requires accurate calibration and creates new data about the user. What looks like a purely technical advantage in this lesson becomes a privacy question in Lesson

11. That pattern runs through the entire course: almost every gain in VR has another side.

The main conclusion of the optics section is simple. A headset does not literally "draw depth." It presents the visual system with a set of signals that resemble those of real space. The better stereoscopy, movement, scale, focus, and field of view agree, the more stable the sense of depth becomes.

The perspective of the virtual camera has to match head position not only in direction, but in scale. If camera parameters are chosen poorly, the world can feel miniature or gigantic. The error is especially obvious near objects of familiar size, because the brain has strong expectations about a door, a chair, a hand, or a cup.

A separate engineering problem comes from the fact that the eyes are not located at one point. Interpupillary distance affects the geometry of the stereo pair. Devices therefore offer IPD adjustment or are designed to work acceptably across a range of users. Mismatched geometry can reduce clarity and comfort even when the person cannot explain exactly what feels wrong.

VR optics are therefore a compromise between the physics of light and the physiology of vision. The display must be compact, the lenses light, the field of view wide enough, the image sharp, and the required computation still manageable. There is no single parameter that can be maximized without cost. This is a common feature of complex technologies: quality comes from balance.

There is another important effect: the brain uses head movement to check depth. When the user shifts slightly, the virtual scene has to respond as a physical scene would. That small amount of parallax can make space more convincing than a simple increase in resolution. This is why 6DoF tracking and stereoscopy work as one system.

Visual comfort also depends on calibration and fit. Fogged lenses, a headset worn too high, or poorly adjusted IPD can produce blur, double vision, or rapid fatigue. These problems remind us that the image passes not only through software but through real optics in front of real eyes.

Modern developers also avoid interfaces that require the user to switch constantly between very near and very distant virtual objects. Such design can increase visual strain. Spatial interfaces have to be designed around the limitations of real eyes, limitations a virtual camera inside an editor does not have.

Photorealism is therefore not the main goal of VR optics. If text is readable, depth is stable, motion is coherent, and the user can work comfortably for a reasonable period, the system can be functionally successful even with stylized graphics. Virtual vision needs to be stable before it needs to be beautiful.

Future display technologies may reduce focus conflict and bring optical cues closer to those of natural vision. But every step demands new computation and usually makes the device more complex. In VR, one advantage is almost always traded for another: wider field of view for weight, sharpness for performance, sophisticated optics for cost.

There is also a practical question of perceived quality. Users often notice not absolute resolution, but whether text is legible, lines remain stable, and the image avoids flicker during movement. Displays are therefore judged in real tasks: can you read small labels, look comfortably at an object off-center, and keep the image sharp as the eyes move?

Optics and rendering work together. Software knows the approximate properties of the lenses and deliberately pre-warps the image so that, after passing through the optical system, it appears more correct. What looks distorted on the raw display may look normal through the lens.

So two small displays become a large space through a chain of processes rather than one trick: two virtual cameras, stereoscopic geometry, lenses, image correction, and head tracking. Break any link and the sense of depth becomes weaker or less stable.

PORTRAIT: CHARLES WHEATSTONE (1802–1875)

English physicist Charles Wheatstone studied binocular vision and in 1838 described the reflecting stereoscope. His experiment showed that differences between the images presented to the two eyes can produce a perception of depth. For the history of VR, this is a fundamental result: a sense of volume can be created not by a physical object, but by carefully organized visual information.

PLOT TWIST: A MODERN HEADSET REPEATS A NINETEENTH-CENTURY PRINCIPLE

High-resolution displays, sensors, and graphics processors belong to the digital age, but the fundamental principle of presenting different images to the two eyes was demonstrated in the nineteenth century.

KEY TERMS

Binocular disparity – the difference between the images of the same scene received by the left and right eyes.

Stereoscopy – the creation of a sense of depth by presenting two different images.

Motion parallax – the change in the apparent position of objects as the observer moves.

Field of view (FOV) – the angular extent of space visible through a device.

Accommodation – the eye's change in focus for objects at different distances.

Vergence – the inward or outward rotation of the eyes when looking at objects at different depths.

Rendering – the computation of the final image of a 3D scene.

TEST

Choose one correct answer.

1. Why are the images shown to the two eyes different?

a) To save energy

b) So one eye can see the menu

c) To increase volume

d) To reproduce the eyes' different viewpoints

2. What is motion parallax?

a) A change in brightness

b) A change in the apparent position of objects as the observer moves

c) A lens error

d) A shift in sound

3. Why does a headset need lenses?

a) To make a nearby display usable for the eyes and form the field of view

b) Only for protection

c) For hand tracking

d) For cooling

4. What does FOV mean?

a) Frame rate

b) Controller type

c) Field of view

d) Video format

5. Which statement about depth is correct?

a) It is determined only by stereoscopy

b) It is possible only during movement

c) It depends only on shadows

d) The brain uses several depth cues

6. What does rendering do?

a) Measures pulse rate

b) Computes an image of the scene

c) Charges the battery

d) Calibrates sound

7. What is accommodation?

a) A change in the eye's focus

b) Head movement

c) Eye convergence

d) Distance measurement by a sensor

8. What is vergence?

a) Focusing by the lens of the eye

b) Lens distortion

c) The inward or outward movement of the eyes when viewing objects at different depths

d) Video compression

9. Why is a stereo pair alone not enough?

a) Smell is required

b) Only music is needed

c) Peripheral vision must be removed

d) The scene must also change consistently with head movement

10. Which limitation is typical of most VR displays?

a) They cannot display color

b) Focal distance does not change as it does in the real world

c) They do not use lenses

d) They do not create perspective

HOME EXPERIMENT

- Look first at a finger held in front of your face, then at a distant object. Notice how the position of your eyes and your sense of focus change. In your "My Virtual World" project, choose three depth cues that matter most to your scene: scale, occlusion, movement, light, or familiar size.
- *In Lesson 4, the image will begin to move with you: we will examine how a headset measures the position of your head and hands.*

LESSON 4. HOW DOES THE HEADSET KNOW HOW YOU ARE MOVING?

SIX WAYS TO MOVE

A rigid body in space can move along three axes and rotate around three axes. That gives us 6DoF, six degrees of freedom. Simpler devices could track only head rotation, or 3DoF. Modern VR usually aims to know both the user's orientation and their position.

The difference is immediate. With 3DoF you can look around, but leaning toward a virtual object does not necessarily change the viewpoint correctly. With 6DoF, the virtual camera moves with your head.

WHAT INERTIAL SENSORS CAN FEEL

A gyroscope measures rotation, while an accelerometer registers acceleration. These sensors report changes in headset motion very quickly. Over longer periods, however, small errors can accumulate.

VR therefore combines several sources of data. Fast inertial measurements are corrected with information from cameras or external references. This is called sensor fusion.

CAMERAS LOOK OUTWARD

Many headsets use inside-out tracking: cameras on the headset observe the surrounding room. The system finds stable features in the scene and estimates its own movement from how those features shift.

Another approach, outside-in tracking, uses external cameras or base stations that observe the headset and controllers. The approaches involve different trade-offs in accuracy, setup convenience, and working area.

HANDS HAVE TO ENTER THE WORLD TOO

Controllers provide buttons, triggers, and points in space that can be tracked reliably. Hand tracking tries to recognize the hands and fingers themselves through cameras. This can make some actions more natural: pointing, pinching, or holding out a palm.

But a hand is harder to track than a controller. Fingers occlude one another, disappear from the cameras' view, and change shape quickly. Natural input therefore requires substantial computer-vision work.

LATENCY BREAKS CAUSALITY

If you turn your head and the virtual world responds noticeably later, space can seem to float or swim. Motion-to-photon latency is critical in VR: it is the time from a user's movement to the corresponding change in light on the display.

Engineers reduce it with fast sensors, high frame rates, motion prediction, and optimized rendering. In Lesson 5, we will see why errors in this loop can cause more than annoyance. They can produce physical discomfort.

HOW TRACKING TURNS A ROOM INTO A COORDINATE SYSTEM

For a virtual object to appear motionless on a table, the headset has to know not only which way the head is turned, but also where it is in relation to the surrounding space. That requires a coordinate system. Inside the software, the positions of the head, controllers, hands, and objects are represented by numbers. When the user takes a step, those numbers change, and the virtual camera must move by a corresponding amount.

Inertial sensors are valuable because they react extremely quickly. A gyroscope senses rotation almost at once, and an accelerometer registers acceleration. But deriving an accurate position from acceleration over a long period is difficult: tiny measurement errors accumulate when integrated. If a VR system relied only on inertial sensing, the virtual world would gradually drift. Cameras help correct that drift by finding stable references in the surrounding environment.

Modern inside-out tracking often uses methods related to visual odometry and SLAM: the system estimates its own motion while also building a working representation of the surrounding geometry. The user does not need to see this map. The device needs it so that it can understand that distinctive points on a wall, cabinet, or floor remain in place while the camera moves. The less texture and contrast a room contains, the harder the problem becomes. A blank, uniform wall offers fewer visual references than a space full of visible detail.

Controllers and hands create a separate problem. The headset must match the positions of objects that may move quickly and temporarily disappear from the cameras' view. If a controller goes behind the user's back, visual tracking may lose it, so the system relies for a while on inertial data and prediction. Hand tracking is harder still: instead of estimating the pose of one rigid body, the system must estimate many joints while fingers repeatedly occlude one another.

Eye tracking adds another coordinate system. Now the device needs to know not only where the head is facing, but where the eyes are directed within the field of view. This can support interfaces, social avatars, and foveated rendering, in which maximum detail is calculated around the current gaze point. When done well, the user does not notice that the peripheral image has been rendered more simply. Once again, a feature of human biology becomes a way to save computation.

Latency ties all these subsystems into one engineering chain. After the head moves, sensors have to detect the movement, an algorithm has to estimate the new pose, the engine has to update the virtual cameras, the graphics processor has to render a frame, and the display has to show it. Every stage takes time. If the total delay becomes too large or inconsistent, cause and effect separate: the person has already turned, while the world is still showing the previous position.

VR systems therefore use prediction. An algorithm estimates where the head will be by the time the frame is actually displayed. This is not fortune-telling, but short-term extrapolation of motion. It works well during smooth turns and less well when movement changes unexpectedly. Other techniques make it possible to correct the image late in the rendering pipeline, when newer pose information is available. Much of VR engineering is a fight for milliseconds.

Tracking also affects safety. A device needs to understand the boundaries of the physical play area so the user does not walk into a wall or a piece of furniture. Modern systems can display a warning when someone approaches the boundary or blend a view of the physical room into the virtual scene. A technology designed to replace the surrounding world therefore has to pay very close attention to the real one. In Lesson 11, this leads to another question: exactly what does the device know about the room and the user, and where is that data processed?

Tracking is closely tied to the idea of a reference frame. In one scene, an object's position may be defined relative to the room; in another, relative to the user; in a third, relative to a moving vehicle. Choosing the wrong coordinate frame creates strange effects: an interface drifts, an object refuses to stay on a table, or a hand appears offset from where it should be.

Developers therefore have to know which objects should be "attached" to the world, which to the head, and which to the hand. A notification panel attached to the head remains in front of the eyes wherever the user turns. The same panel anchored in the room stays in one place when the user looks away. This is not a small detail. It is part of how space is experienced.

Inside-out tracking depends on the quality of the surrounding scene. A very dark room, mirrors, uniform surfaces, or rapidly changing lighting can make the cameras' job harder. Modern systems are robust under many conditions, but the principle remains: the device estimates movement from the information its sensors can obtain.

Hand tracking has another engineering cost: the system must do more than locate the hand. It has to estimate a hand skeleton, meaning the positions of many joints. Those data then have to be smoothed so that virtual fingers do not jitter, but without adding noticeable delay. Too much smoothing makes motion feel sticky; too little reveals measurement noise.

Eye tracking faces a similar trade-off. The eyes move very quickly, and the system must distinguish useful gaze direction from tiny eye movements and blinks. The resulting data can then be used for object selection, rendering, or avatar animation. A single sensor may serve several functions at once.

Ultimately, tracking determines how much the user trusts the virtual world. If an object on a table trembles slightly every time the head moves, the user quickly realizes that the "table" is not where it should be. Good tracking is almost invisible. Its quality appears in the absence of events: the world does not drift, hands do not detach, and objects keep their places. In VR engineering, invisible stability often matters more than a spectacular feature.

Tracking is needed for more than head movement. It determines how well a system can combine virtual and real objects. If a digital object is meant to sit on a physical table, an error in pose estimation becomes a visible offset. The closer VR moves toward mixed reality, the stricter the requirements for a shared geometry of the world.

The system also has to recognize when tracking has been lost. A controller can disappear behind the user's back, a camera can be covered by a hand, or the room can become too dark. A good product does not pretend that the measurement is still precise. It may freeze the object carefully, rely on prediction, inform the user about the problem, or switch to another safe mode.

Tracking makes the difference between a laboratory demonstration and a consumer product especially clear. In a lab, researchers can prepare an ideal room and install many sensors. A consumer headset has to work in a bedroom, office, or living room, under different lighting and around different furniture. A mass-market system needs not only high accuracy, but resilience to ordinary life.

Real-time tracking is also tied to the map of physical boundaries. The user's body can move only within the room, while the virtual world may be enormous. Applications therefore combine physical walking with artificial locomotion. This is our first example of the geometry of the real room limiting digital freedom.

Some methods try to use that boundary creatively. Redirected walking subtly alters the virtual scene so that a person physically turns a little more or less than they realize and remains inside the available area. These techniques are interesting in research, but they require caution because they work through subtle features of motion perception.

Tracking stability becomes especially important when the user interacts with physical objects. If a mixed-reality application places a virtual keyboard on a real table, even a small offset is immediately obvious to the hand. The more a system promises to merge digital and physical objects, the less geometric error it can tolerate.

Developers also have to decide what happens when a real boundary is crossed. The system might display a grid, turn on passthrough, stop locomotion, or sound a warning. A good solution needs to be noticeable without being alarming and should trigger before a collision occurs.

Tracking thus gradually stops being merely a way to "look around." It becomes the infrastructure of a spatial computer: it locates the person, the hands, the room, and digital objects within one coordinate system. Every later lesson builds on that infrastructure.

Modern tracking also helps a device understand the floor and the user's height. Those estimates affect where a virtual surface appears and whether crouching or leaning looks natural. An error of only a few centimeters can make a virtual hand pass through a table or give the user the wrong sense of their own height.

Calibration, then, is not boring setup. It is part of the geometry of the experience. The system has to establish an initial pose, the boundaries of the area, and sometimes the position of the eyes.

The less visible this process is to the user, the better the product feels, but the engineering need does not disappear.

Tracking ultimately creates a continuous link between the body and the coordinates of the digital scene. That link turns 3D graphics from a picture you can inspect into a space in which you can act.

Tracking must remain stable not only during an ordinary head turn, but also during quick tilts, crouches, and hand movements close to the headset cameras. Edge cases often expose the weak points of a system. Testing therefore includes more than standing calmly. It includes movements a real user may make unexpectedly. The more reliable tracking is in those situations, the less often a person remembers that the virtual world is being held together by measurements.

PORTRAIT: JARON LANIER (1960–)

American computer scientist and musician Jaron Lanier worked in the 1980s at VPL Research, which developed early commercial VR systems including gloves and head-mounted displays. His name is often associated with popularizing the expression virtual reality. Lanier later became a critic of some directions taken by the digital industry, so his biography connects early technological optimism with questions about the consequences of digital mediation.

PLOT TWIST: A HEADSET IS CONSTANTLY SOLVING THE PROBLEM OF WHERE IT IS

The user sees a stable world only because the device estimates its own movement many times a second. When that invisible geometric problem is solved badly, the scene begins to shake, drift, or lag.

KEY TERMS

6DoF – six degrees of freedom: three translations and three rotations.

Gyroscope – a sensor that measures rotational motion.

Accelerometer – a sensor that measures acceleration.

Inside-out tracking – tracking performed with cameras and sensors on the device itself.

Outside-in tracking – tracking in which external cameras or stations observe the device.

Sensor fusion – the combination of several sources of motion data.

Motion-to-photon latency – the time between a user's movement and the corresponding change in the displayed image.

TEST

Choose one correct answer.

1. What does 6DoF include?

a) Three translations and three rotations

b) Only three rotations

c) Six cameras

d) Six controllers

2. What does a gyroscope measure?

a) Wall color

b) Pulse rate

c) Rotational motion

d) Distance to a server

3. Why combine sensors and cameras?

a) To increase volume

b) To disable rendering

c) To remove stereoscopy

d) To compensate for the weaknesses of different data sources

. . .

4. What is inside-out tracking?

a) External cameras observe the headset

b) The headset estimates its position with its own cameras

c) Tracking only the eyes

d) Sending video outward

5. Why are fingers difficult to track?

a) They change shape and occlude one another

b) They do not move

c) Cameras cannot see skin

d) They move only together

6. What does latency mean?

a) Resolution

b) Field of view

c) Delay

d) Color depth

7. Why is latency especially noticeable in VR?

a) The user is always running

b) The headset turns off sound

c) The eyes cannot see movement

d) The image must update quickly to match head movement

8. What does an accelerometer do?

a) Builds a 3D model

b) Measures acceleration

c) Displays the image

d) Detects color

9. What does 3DoF lack compared with 6DoF?

a) Full tracking of position in space

b) Sound output

c) Separate images for two eyes

d) The ability to turn on

10. What keeps the virtual world stable?

a) The heaviest possible headset

b) Brightness alone

c) An accurate, fast link between movement and scene updates

d) The internet alone

HOME EXPERIMENT

- If your phone has a compass or orientation display, turn the device slowly and then quickly and watch how the readings change. In your "My Virtual World" project, choose a locomotion method: physical walking, teleportation, joystick movement, or a combination. Explain why you chose it.
- *The system now knows how you are moving. In Lesson 5, we will examine a paradox: why convincing virtual motion can sometimes make the body protest.*

LESSON 5. WHY CAN VIRTUAL REALITY MAKE YOU FEEL SICK?

WHEN THE EYES AND INNER EAR DISAGREE

Cybersickness can include nausea, dizziness, eye strain, headache, and disorientation. There is no single theory that explains every case. One of the leading ideas involves sensory conflict: vision reports movement while the vestibular system does not detect the corresponding acceleration.

For example, a person may be standing still while the virtual camera glides forward. Vision says movement; the inner ear says rest. The body receives an unusual combination of signals.

IT IS NOT JUST THE HARDWARE

High latency, unstable frame rates, and tracking errors can make people feel worse. But the content of the scene matters too. Fast virtual rotation, movement without a physical step, and unexpected acceleration are often harder to tolerate than calm interaction in place.

People differ in sensitivity, so there is no universal safe session length. Good design offers comfortable ways to move and never requires users to endure symptoms.

WHY TELEPORTATION BECAME NORMAL

Teleportation sounds strange only until you use VR. The user points to a location and moves there instantly. This breaks up continuous visual motion and often reduces sensory conflict.

Another technique, snap turn, rotates the scene in discrete steps. Some systems temporarily narrow the field of view during rapid movement. Here, the user's physiology literally shapes the interface.

ADAPTATION IS NOT A UNIVERSAL CURE

Some people become more tolerant of particular scenes over time, but "just push through it" is poor advice. Strong symptoms are a reason to stop the session or change the conditions. Research on cybersickness is ongoing, and devices, content, and users differ greatly.

Medical uses require particular caution. Personal experience with a headset is not a substitute for a clinical protocol or an assessment of side effects.

COMFORT AS AN ENGINEERING REQUIREMENT

In an ordinary game, a bad camera is irritating. In VR, it can make an application physically intolerable. Comfort is therefore part of functionality.

Engineers and designers have to consider the vestibular system, field of view, frame rate, posture, and locomotion method. In the next lesson we will start building the scene itself and see why visual beauty always competes with the computing budget.

WHY ONE USER FEELS FINE AND ANOTHER DOES NOT

Cybersickness is awkward to explain because it cannot be reduced to a single parameter. You cannot say, "above this frame rate, the problem disappears" or "everyone simply needs time to adapt." Symptoms are influenced by the device, the scenario, session length, type of movement, individual sensitivity, and even whether the person is actively performing a task or passively riding along a virtual path.

Sensory conflict remains one of the main explanations. During ordinary walking, vision, the inner ear, and signals from the muscles all report movement in a coordinated way. If the virtual camera travels forward while the body stands still, that agreement breaks. Acceleration and rotation can be especially difficult because the vestibular system normally senses them strongly in the real world. The virtual scene reports an event that the body does not confirm.

That theory does not explain everything. Other accounts focus on failures of postural control: discomfort may arise when an unusual sensory situation makes it harder to maintain stable posture. Researchers still debate how well different mechanisms explain different symptoms. The scientifically honest point is this: cybersickness is real and well documented, but there is no single complete explanation for every case.

Content matters enormously. If a virtual car accelerates sharply, the user sees strong acceleration. If the camera rotates around its own axis without a matching bodily movement, the conflict becomes particularly obvious. Developers therefore often offer several locomotion modes. One person prefers smooth joystick movement; another chooses teleportation. A good interface does not declare one style "correct" for everyone.

Scale and the horizon matter as well. A stable visual reference can help some users, while a chaotic camera makes orientation harder. A cockpit in a simulator can therefore be useful for more than storytelling: because it remains stable relative to the user, the cockpit gives the visual system a fixed frame of reference. Other applications temporarily narrow peripheral vision during motion, reducing the amount of optic flow.

Technical performance should not be judged only by an average such as "it is usually fast." Stability matters. Occasional frame drops, tracking jolts, and spikes in latency can be especially unpleasant because they break the predictability of the relationship between the head and the scene. In VR, a merely adequate but steady system may feel better than one that is excellent most of the time and then suddenly stutters.

User safety also includes simple physical realities. After a session, a person may need a short moment to reorient fully to the room. A headset blocks the view of real obstacles. A controller can strike furniture. Play-area boundaries, passthrough modes, and warnings are therefore safety features, not secondary conveniences.

When VR is used for treatment, patient education, or rehabilitation, medical risks enter the picture. Studies need to report adverse effects as well as benefits. Systematic reviews have noted that publications have not always documented adverse events with the same care. This is an important reminder: a technology can be useful and still require careful safety monitoring.

For our course project, the practical conclusion is simple: comfort must be designed from the beginning. You cannot build a spectacular world first and add a "comfort mode" at the end. Locomotion, interaction frequency, object placement, horizon stability, and the ability to stop should be discussed alongside the core mechanics. In VR, the user's physiology belongs in the technical brief.

Research on cybersickness offers another practical lesson: never judge comfort only by your own response. A developer who wears a headset every day may adapt to a scene and stop noticing problems that are obvious to a newcomer. VR should therefore be tested on different people, with attention not only to complaints but to the conditions in which they appear.

Scenes in which movement begins without the user's initiative can be particularly troublesome. When a person presses a controller and expects to move, the causal link is clearer. If the camera suddenly moves on its own, the brain receives an unexpected visual event. One useful rule follows: whenever possible, the user should control the movement of their own viewpoint.

Pacing matters too. Sharp acceleration and rotation are generally harder to tolerate than slower motion. But an excessively slow system can become frustrating and force the user into unnecessary actions. Comfortable design is not simply "make everything slower." It seeks predictable movement and offers a clear alternative.

Cybersickness should also be distinguished from fatigue. A heavy headset can press on the face, the eyes can tire from prolonged viewing, and the arms can tire from holding a pose. These problems need different solutions, even though a user may describe all of them with the same word, "uncomfortable." Good testing records more specific symptoms.

Finally, a commercial technology should not hide its limits. If an application uses intense artificial motion, the user should know before the session begins. A quick way to exit, sit down, change locomotion mode, or view the real room makes the system safer. In VR, respect for the user's body is part of product quality.

Cybersickness also matters because it limits access to the technology. If some users cannot comfortably tolerate a popular form of movement, the application effectively excludes them. Locomotion is therefore a question of inclusion as well as convenience. The option to sit, turn in steps, or disable intense effects allows more people to use the system.

Adaptation has a downside too. A developer who is highly accustomed to VR may underestimate the experience of a newcomer. Testing should therefore include people with different levels of experience and should never encourage them to hide symptoms just to finish a task. Accurate observation matters more than endurance.

Cybersickness thus connects physiology, design, and ethics. A system must do more than function technically. It must give a person control over their own physical state. This is a rare case in which bodily well-being becomes a direct metric of interface quality.

Researchers study cybersickness with symptom questionnaires, behavioral observation, and physiological measures, but no single method gives a complete answer. A person may report mild discomfort that does not interfere with the task, or may stop a session before severe nausea develops. Evaluation therefore has to consider both subjective experience and whether the person can continue.

Symptoms can also accumulate. The first few minutes may feel fine, followed by eye fatigue or dizziness later. A comfortable five-minute demonstration does not prove that a one-hour training session will be equally comfortable. Duration is part of the design.

Age, experience, health, and individual susceptibility may affect response, but there is no simple profile that tells us who will definitely become ill. Designers should not assume that a sensitive user simply "does not belong" in the product. Better options are settings, alternatives, and an easy way to stop safely.

Context matters as well. Someone performing an active task may experience movement differently from a passive passenger on a virtual ride. Control over action makes the sensory consequences more predictable. This is another reason to give users control over their own camera whenever possible.

Cybersickness reminds us that visual design and bodily design meet in VR. In an ordinary interface, bad animation is irritating. In VR, a similar error can affect balance and physical comfort. The standard for motion quality is therefore genuinely higher.

Developers sometimes provide comfort ratings or warn users in advance about the type of locomotion involved. Such information helps people choose an experience according to their own sensitivity. This is especially sensible when intense motion is integral to the design and cannot simply be removed.

It is also important to distinguish short-term adaptation from safe use. If a person becomes more tolerant after several sessions, that does not mean every newcomer should first endure strong symptoms. Comfortable design lowers the barrier to entry rather than turning discomfort into a test of toughness.

Cybersickness remains one of VR's main constraints and, at the same time, a source of engineering solutions. Teleportation, snap turn, stable horizons, and user-controlled movement did not appear as aesthetic fashions. They emerged in response to human perception.

Comfort can shape content too. A creator may abandon a spectacular virtual ride if it is not necessary for the task and keep the action in one place instead. That is not a creative defeat but a good use of the medium. In VR, the most effective movement is not the most movement, but movement whose meaning is clear to both the user and the body. Physiological limits often improve a project by forcing designers to remove unnecessary spectacle and keep what matters.

The return to the physical environment matters as well. After an intense session, the user should remove the headset calmly, make sure they are oriented, and only then move around. This is especially relevant after applications with a great deal of artificial locomotion. A good experience ends as carefully as it begins: no abrupt cut, no pressure to continue, and a clear option to stop at the first sign of discomfort.

Comfort cannot be reduced to one average number for all users. It is more useful to offer choices, explain the nature of the movement, and let the user change modes without losing progress. Such flexibility does not weaken the creative intent. It makes the experience accessible to more people. In VR, respect for individual bodily response is as basic a requirement as a button that works or an object that stays where it belongs.

PORTRAIT: JAMES J. GIBSON (1904–1979)

American psychologist James J. Gibson studied visual perception and the way an observer's movement changes the structure of visual information. His concept of optical flow predates modern VR headsets by decades, but it helps explain something essential: vision tells the brain not only about objects, but also about the observer's own movement. When a virtual scene produces a strong motion signal while the body remains still, that connection becomes especially visible.

PLOT TWIST: MORE REALISTIC DOES NOT ALWAYS MEAN MORE COMFORTABLE

Smooth camera flight may feel natural to a developer but be less comfortable for a stationary user than an artificial teleport. VR repeatedly forces a choice between cinematic smoothness and physiological consistency.

KEY TERMS

Cybersickness – unpleasant symptoms experienced by some VR users.

Vestibular system – the inner-ear and brain systems involved in sensing movement and balance.

Sensory conflict – disagreement among information coming from different senses.

Snap turn – rotation of the virtual scene in discrete steps.

Teleportation – instant movement of the user to a selected point.

Frame rate – the number of displayed frames per second.

Comfort mode – a set of design choices intended to reduce the risk of discomfort.

TEST

Choose one correct answer.

1. What is cybersickness?

a) A computer error

b) Fear of the internet

c) A set of unpleasant symptoms associated with VR

d) A broken controller

2. What is sensory conflict?

a) Low audio volume

b) The absence of an avatar

c) Weak Wi-Fi

d) Disagreement among signals from different senses

3. Why can virtual flight cause discomfort?

a) Vision reports motion without corresponding bodily motion

b) The screen turns black

c) The controller vibrates

d) The eyes stop seeing depth

. . .

4. Why is teleportation used?

a) To increase the polygon count

b) To reduce continuous visual motion

c) To turn off tracking

d) To replace sound

5. What is snap turn?

a) Smooth rotation

b) Finger tracking

c) Rotation in discrete steps

d) Changing the avatar

6. Is there one final theory of cybersickness?

a) Yes

b) Only for children

c) Only in games

d) No

7. What should a user do if significant discomfort develops?

a) Stop or change the session

b) Endure it until the end

c) Increase the speed

d) Close one eye

8. What besides hardware can affect symptoms?

a) The color of the headset shell

b) The content and type of movement

c) The price of the device

d) The age of the application

9. Why is comfort part of functionality?

a) It affects only the menu

b) The internet will not work without it

c) Poor design can cause physical symptoms

d) It matters only to beginners

10. What does Lesson 5 lead into?

a) Building a scene under limited computing resources

b) The history of the stereoscope

c) Printing technology

d) Keyboards

HOME EXPERIMENT

- Do not deliberately provoke discomfort. Watch an ordinary video with a moving camera and note which kinds of camera movement feel calm and which feel unpleasant. In your project, decide which locomotion method will be the default for a beginner and which comfortable alternative will remain available.
- *In Lesson 6, we will open the virtual world from the developer's side and see which computable pieces it is made from.*

LESSON 6. WHAT IS A VIRTUAL WORLD MADE OF?

A SCENE BEGINS WITH GEOMETRY

For a computer, a virtual room begins not with wood and glass, but with a mathematical description of shape. Most 3D objects are built from a polygon mesh: vertices, edges, and faces. The more complex the shape, the more data the system has to process.

Polygon count alone does not determine quality. A good model spends detail where the user will notice it and saves resources where the difference is barely visible.

A MATERIAL IS MORE THAN A COLOR

Surfaces receive textures and materials. A texture can define color and fine detail, while a material describes how a surface interacts with light: whether it is shiny, rough, transparent, and so on.

Lighting ties objects into one space. Incorrect lighting can destroy the sense of scale even when the models are good, especially because a VR user can walk up to an object and inspect it from an unexpected angle.

THE WORLD HAS TO BE REDRAWN IN TIME

The computer builds a separate image for each eye and repeats the process many times every second. If the scene is too demanding, the frame rate drops and comfort suffers. Developers therefore use levels of detail, simplified models, precomputed lighting, and other optimization techniques.

A photorealistic detail is useless if it makes the image lag behind the user's head.

PHYSICS IS SOFTWARE TOO

If a virtual cube falls, there is no real gravity inside the headset. A physics engine calculates the motion according to programmed rules. Colliders define collision boundaries, while mass and forces influence how objects behave.

A developer can imitate real physics or deliberately break it. What matters is that the rules of the world remain consistent and understandable to the user.

SOUND BUILDS INVISIBLE GEOMETRY

Spatial audio helps you tell where a source is: right, left, above, or behind. When the head turns, the audio scene has to update with the visual one. Sound then confirms that objects exist outside the current field of view.

In good VR, sound is not decoration added after the graphics. It directs attention and helps the user orient themselves.

THE ENGINE AS AN ASSEMBLY FLOOR

Unity and Unreal Engine are widely used to assemble interactive scenes: developers define objects, behavior, input, physics, sound, and rendering. Blender is often used to create 3D models. Particular software changes over time, but the logic remains: create a model, place it in a scene, give it materials and behavior, then optimize it for the target device.

HOW A SCENE TRAVELS FROM A MODEL TO THE IMAGE BEFORE YOUR EYES

It is useful to imagine a VR scene as a stack of layers. First comes geometry. Then surfaces receive materials. Lights are added to the scene. Objects are assigned behavior and physical properties. Finally, the engine must calculate how everything looks from the viewpoint of each eye and send the frames to the display. Any layer can become a performance bottleneck.

A polygon model is only an approximation of shape. A round object is actually made from many flat faces, but with a sufficiently dense mesh and good lighting, the eye stops noticing the approximation. Developers choose where extra polygons are worth spending. A bolt on a distant machine can be simplified; a hand close to the user's face needs much more care.

Textures can save geometry. Fine scratches, the weave of fabric, or brickwork can be represented partly through images and specialized maps rather than modeled as separate three-dimensional details. A material tells the engine how a surface reflects light. Modern systems often use physically based rendering so that wood, metal, plastic, and skin respond to lighting in a consistent way.

Real-time lighting is expensive to calculate. In a static scene, some lighting can be computed in advance and stored. A dynamic light source, by contrast, requires ongoing calculations, especially if it casts shadows. The cost rises in VR because images have to be generated for two eyes at a high, stable frame rate. Developers are constantly deciding which effects the user will actually notice.

Levels of detail, or LODs, take advantage of distance. When an object is far away, the system shows a simplified model. As the user approaches, it swaps in a more detailed one. Ideally, the transition goes unnoticed. A similar principle applies to visibility: there is no reason to render in detail what is behind a wall or outside the current view. Such techniques spend computation where it becomes visible quality.

The physics engine uses simplifications too. A visually detailed object may use a much simpler collider for collisions. That is sensible: the user's finger needs the cup to stay on the table, not every curve of the cup to participate in the collision calculation. The more interactive objects a scene contains, the more important it becomes to separate visual shape from physics shape.

Sound adds another model of space. To determine direction, the system takes head position and properties of human hearing into account. More advanced solutions can model reflections and attenuation behind obstacles. Even simple spatial localization is useful: if a bell rings behind you, you turn before you see its source. Sound extends the scene beyond the current gaze.

A game engine combines all these layers. It does not "create VR with one button." Developers still have to build the scene and configure cameras, input, interactions, and performance. Modern XR frameworks help support different headsets and input methods, but they do not eliminate design work. Tools standardize part of the technical foundation so that a team can devote more attention to the experience itself.

Thinking in budgets is especially useful. There are budgets for polygons, lighting, memory, CPU time, GPU time, and network traffic. Every attractive feature consumes something. In an offline visualization, you can wait several seconds for a beautiful frame. In VR, you cannot. The user is moving now, and the image has to respond now. Real skill often appears when a world feels richer than its computing budget should allow.

VR performance is better judged not by the beauty of one frame, but by the system's ability to maintain quality during movement. A screenshot may look magnificent, but the user experiences the world over time. If frames arrive unevenly when the head turns, a beautiful still image cannot preserve presence.

That is why developers profile their applications. They measure how much time is spent by the CPU, GPU, physics, animation, and scripts. Optimization begins not with randomly deleting details, but with finding the real bottleneck. Otherwise, a team can damage the scene and gain almost no performance.

Distance to an object matters greatly. A detail the user can never see up close does not need the same complexity as an object held in the hands. This is especially important in VR, where the user has more freedom than a camera in a conventional game. The team needs to know in advance which objects can be approached and which can be picked up.

Interactivity changes model requirements too. A decorative box may be one simple shape. A box that opens needs separate parts, colliders, a grab point, animation, and sound. The cost of an object is therefore determined not only by how it looks, but by what the user is allowed to do with it.

Physical realism can also be used selectively. Sometimes an exact simulation is unnecessary, and a simplified motion explains the task better. In an educational scene, a process can be slowed down, an effect can be exaggerated, or secondary factors can be removed. The simplification should be deliberate and should not create a false understanding.

A virtual world is therefore built from continual choices. Where should polygons be spent? What should be precomputed? Which sounds matter? Which physics are essential? What will the user see and touch? A good scene does not contain the maximum possible technology. It contains the technologies that support the purpose of the experience.

In VR, it is particularly useful to distinguish what the user sees from what the system calculates. A beautiful sword may contain thousands of visual details but use a simple collision shape. A room may appear to be lit by dozens of lamps even though some of its light has been baked into textures. This mismatch is not deception. It is engineering economy.

A scene also contains invisible service objects: spawn points, interaction zones, event triggers, navigation areas, and safety boundaries. They do not exist for the eye, but they determine how the world behaves. VR development resembles theater in this respect: a complex mechanism is hidden behind the visible set.

The more freedom the user has, the more complicated that mechanism becomes. If a person can walk behind an object, look under a table, and throw something into an unexpected place, the creator has to account for more states than in a scene with a fixed camera. User freedom increases both the impact and the cost of development.

Virtual scenes are often built by teams. A 3D artist handles models and materials, a programmer handles behavior, a technical artist balances quality and performance, a sound designer builds the audio space, and a UX designer tests interaction. The roles overlap because a change in one layer affects the others.

An artist, for example, may add a transparent material that looks beautiful but is expensive to render. A programmer may build realistic physics that becomes unstable under frequent interaction. A good team discusses such constraints early instead of repairing them at the end.

Coordinate systems and units are critical too. If one model is imported in meters and another in centimeters, the virtual world quickly loses its sense of scale. On a monitor, such an error may go unnoticed. In VR, the human body provides a constant measuring stick.

Optimization begins by watching a real user. If nobody ever comes within two meters of a wall, there is little reason to spend a huge budget on microscopic plaster detail. If an object is constantly held close to the face, cutting detail there will be obvious.

Building a VR world is therefore less like painting one perfect image and more like designing a scene that has to survive human movement, curiosity, and unpredictability.

Scene assets must also fit into device memory. High-quality textures, complex models, and sound take space, and a standalone headset has tighter limits than a powerful workstation. Teams therefore think not only about rendering speed, but about asset size.

Repeated objects can use instancing and other techniques that avoid storing or calculating the same work over and over. Distant objects use simplified versions. Lighting is divided between what can be precomputed and what must be calculated in real time.

All these methods serve one goal: to preserve the illusion of a rich world within finite resources. Virtual reality exists inside a computing budget, and a developer's talent often shows in the ability to spend that budget where the user will truly see the difference.

Testing on the actual device is essential because an editor running on a powerful computer does not reveal the real cost of every effect. Something that runs smoothly on a workstation may be too demanding for a standalone headset. Development therefore proceeds in a cycle: build, measure, simplify, test again. Optimization is not final cleanup. It is a continuous part of VR production.

Even scene loading belongs to the experience. If a world appears slowly in pieces or an object suddenly pops into existence in front of the user, presence is disrupted. Assets are therefore prepared, preloaded, and distributed across stages. In VR, performance means more than a high FPS. It means predictable behavior from launch through interaction.

PORTRAIT: IVAN SUTHERLAND (1938–)

Sutherland appears in this course a second time for a reason. His early work in interactive graphics helps explain the difference between a virtual world and a film. The computer stores the structure of objects and recalculates their appearance from a new viewpoint. That idea connects Sketchpad, the first head-mounted displays, and modern game engines.

PLOT TWIST: THE MOST EXPENSIVE DETAIL MAY BE THE ONE THE USER NEVER NOTICES

A great deal of VR development is spent removing what is unnecessary: invisible polygons, effects that cost too much to render, and calculations that do not need to be made. Optimization succeeds precisely when the user does not notice it.

KEY TERMS

Polygon mesh – a set of vertices, edges, and faces that defines the shape of a 3D object.

Texture – data that defines surface detail on a model.

Material – a description of how a surface interacts with light.

Collider – geometry used to calculate collisions.

Physics engine – a system that calculates motion, collisions, and forces.

Optimization – modification of a scene to achieve stable performance.

Game engine – a software environment for assembling interactive 3D scenes.

Spatial audio – sound that conveys the direction and position of its source.

TEST

Choose one correct answer.

1. What is normally used to define the shape of a 3D object?

a) Photographs alone

b) A polygon mesh

c) Sounds

d) Text

2. What does a material describe?

a) Only an object's name

b) The user's position

c) How a surface behaves under lighting

d) Network latency

3. Why does VR require optimization?

a) To make the controller smaller

b) To turn off sound

c) To remove interactivity

d) The scene must be drawn quickly for two eyes while the head is moving

4. What does a collider do?

a) Defines the collision region

b) Draws a texture

c) Records a voice

d) Measures gaze

5. Why is physics in VR computational?

a) Objects really fall inside the headset

b) The computer calculates behavior according to rules

c) Physics comes from the camera

d) The eyes create it

6. Why use spatial audio?

a) Only to increase volume

b) To reduce polygon count

c) To help locate sound sources

d) To replace rendering

. . .

7. What is a game engine?

a) Only a drawing program

b) A headset model

c) A type of sensor

d) An environment for assembling interactive scenes

8. What is commonly used for 3D modeling?

a) Blender

b) Only a web browser

c) A text editor

d) A calculator

9. What matters more than polygon count by itself?

a) Always using the maximum possible number of polygons

b) Allocating detail where it matters

c) Using as little light as possible

d) Avoiding materials

10. What can happen if a scene is too demanding?

a) The room grows larger

b) Stereoscopy disappears permanently

c) The frame rate drops

d) All sensors stop

HOME EXPERIMENT

- Analyze your room like a developer. Name five objects, two surface materials, two light sources, and three sounds. Then make the same list for "My Virtual World." Keep only the details without which the place would lose its meaning.
- *In Lesson 7, we will see why building a beautiful room is not enough. The user also has to understand what they can do there.*

LESSON 7. WHY ISN'T A BEAUTIFUL VIRTUAL WORLD ENOUGH?

A DOOR HAS TO EXPLAIN ITSELF

In the physical world, objects carry familiar cues. A handle shows where to pull; a button invites a press. In VR, some of those cues disappear or become ambiguous. A beautiful cabinet is useless if the user cannot tell whether it opens or what movement will open it.

Interaction design connects human intention with system response. Good VR does not make the user guess the rules at every step.

CONTROLLER, HAND, OR GAZE

The same choice can be made with a controller button, a finger gesture, gaze, or virtual touch. A controller is precise and provides physical buttons. Hand tracking can feel more natural, but it struggles when fingers occlude one another and provides no real resistance. Gaze is convenient for aiming, but risky as the only confirmation because people often look without intending to select.

FEEDBACK COMPLETES THE ACTION

A real button moves and pushes back against your finger. In VR, the system has to tell you that an action has been registered. An object can change position, a click can sound, a controller can vibrate, or a visual response can appear.

Without feedback, users repeat actions and lose confidence in the system. Interaction works like a short dialogue: intention, action, response.

WHERE SHOULD THE MENU GO?

On a monitor, interface elements fit naturally around the edges of a rectangular screen. In VR, there is almost no stable frame. A menu can be anchored in space, attached to the hand, summoned in front of the user, or built into objects in the world.

A panel placed too close gets in the way; one placed too far away becomes unreadable. Spatial interfaces have to account for distance, text size, and natural head movement.

THE USER CAN LOOK ANYWHERE

Cinema controls the frame. VR gives part of that control to the viewer. A director cannot be sure the user is looking where an event occurs. Sound, light, character movement, and composition therefore become gentle guides for attention.

Instead of one frame, we get an environment in which an important event has to remain discoverable from several directions.

WHY THE MOST NATURAL ACTION IS NOT ALWAYS THE BEST INTERFACE

The intuitive dream of VR sounds simple: if the space is three-dimensional, let the user do everything exactly as they would in real life. In practice, literal copies of physical actions are often inconvenient. A real door pushes back against the hand, a mug has weight, and a keyboard supports the fingers. Those signals are absent in empty air. A supposedly "natural" gesture can therefore be less understandable than a conventional button.

Consider grabbing an object. In the real world, the fingers wrap around it and feel contact. With a controller, the user can press a trigger and the system can attach the object to the virtual hand. That is a convention, but it is stable and provides a physical button. Hand tracking looks more natural, yet the user cannot feel weight and the camera may lose part of the hand. The designer chooses not the most realistic method, but the one that best serves the task.

The idea of affordance is especially important for virtual objects. If a door handle looks graspable, the user expects to be able to grasp it. If it is decorative and does nothing, the world violates that expectation. If an object is interactive but looks no different from the scenery, the user may miss it. Visual design, animation, sound, and placement therefore need to communicate possible actions without a long instruction manual.

Feedback works on several levels. First, the user needs to know that the system noticed the action. Then that the action is allowed. Then what result occurred. Hovering might highlight an object, grabbing might change the hand pose, and releasing might produce a collision sound. When each stage answers clearly, controls feel reliable even if the underlying mechanic is conventional rather than physically literal.

VR is especially sensitive to interface scale. Text that works well on a monitor can be too small or too close to the eyes in a headset. A panel fixed in front of the face moves with the head and can become tiring. Interfaces are therefore often placed as part of the environment: a control panel on a wall, a watch on the wrist, or a menu on a virtual tablet. A digital function gains a comprehensible place in space.

Accessibility matters too. Not every user can stand for long periods, raise their arms high, rotate the torso quickly, or perform gestures with equal precision. Good systems provide alternatives: seated mode, height adjustment, a button instead of a gesture, subtitles, speed controls, and different locomotion methods. Accessibility is closely tied to overall interface quality because human bodies vary widely.

Directing attention in VR is harder than in film. Forcing the virtual camera to turn is usually a poor solution: it takes control away from the user and can cause discomfort. Designers therefore use spatial cues. A character looks toward the important place. A sound comes from behind a door. Light draws attention to an object. Movement appears in the periphery. These methods preserve freedom while making it more likely that the user will notice the event.

Social interfaces introduce new rules. A gesture that feels neutral to one person may feel unpleasant to another. Distance between avatars affects personal space. Interaction design therefore includes not only the manipulation of objects, but norms of behavior among people. A virtual environment becomes a place, and places need rules.

The main criterion remains simple: the user should understand what they can do, know that the system understood the action, and see what happened next. If achieving that requires a convention instead of physical realism, the convention may be the better design. VR is interesting precisely because realism is a tool, not an obligation.

There is another reason VR interfaces need their own design: the user's body has limits. Holding the arms out in front for long periods is tiring, an effect sometimes described as "gorilla arm" in discussions of vertical touch interfaces. Frequently used controls are therefore best placed where they can be reached without constant shoulder strain.

Text in space has to remain readable while the head moves. Type that is too small forces the user to lean closer; an overly wide block is difficult to take in at a glance. VR interfaces therefore tend to use short phrases, large elements, and a clear hierarchy. Long-form reading is possible, but it demands especially careful placement.

Gestures need to be learnable. A developer can invent dozens of elegant finger combinations, but users do not know them in advance. A good gesture vocabulary is small, distinct, and supported by cues. If recognition errors look like user errors, trust disappears quickly.

Gaze interaction needs the principle "looking does not mean agreeing." Gaze can move a pointer, while confirmation comes from a pinch, a button, or a deliberate dwell. This reduces accidental actions and makes intention explicit.

Accessibility extends the same logic. A user may have a limited range of motion, hear less well, remain seated instead of standing, or use one hand. Alternative input benefits more than a narrow group. It makes the product more robust across different circumstances.

A good VR interface therefore rarely looks like a showcase for the maximum possible number of gestures. It creates the impression that the system understands the person with minimal effort. The less attention the user spends thinking about controls, the more attention remains for the actual task.

A good interface is consistent as well. If one drawer opens by grabbing its handle while the next requires an unexplained button press, the user has to memorize exceptions. Consistent rules let a person transfer what they learned from one object to another and reduce the need for instructions.

System errors should be distinguished from user errors. If hand tracking is lost, the interface should not behave as though the user performed the wrong gesture. Developers use visual indications of confidence, repeated recognition, and safe fallback states so that a technical failure does not become a punishment.

In the end, the naturalness of an interface is determined not by how closely it copies reality, but by how quickly a person forms a correct model of the action. Sometimes a physically realistic gesture wins. Sometimes a conventional button is clearer. VR design begins when the creator stops asking "What looks more impressive?" and starts asking "What will the user understand without extra explanation?"

The interface also has to account for recognition errors. If the system sometimes interprets an accidental movement as a command, the user needs a way to undo the action. Undo, confirmation for risky operations, and protection against accidental selection matter in VR just as much as on an ordinary computer.

Good design makes use of spatial memory. Users remember that tools are on the left, the map is on the wall, and settings are on a virtual wrist. If elements constantly jump around the space, that memory is destroyed. Stable placement reduces cognitive load.

Interactive objects also need to be distinguishable from scenery. That does not mean outlining everything in neon. The environment simply needs clear cues. Sometimes the shape of a handle is enough; sometimes a subtle highlight on hover is needed; sometimes a brief prompt is useful the first time.

Sound often serves as confirmation. A click, a mechanical impact, or a short tone can communicate a successful action faster than a text box. Vibration adds another channel. Several modest signals working together usually feel more natural than one loud warning.

A VR interface is therefore designed as the behavior of space. The user does not read it only with the eyes, but explores it through body position, distance, and movement. Familiar principles of screen-based UX are not discarded; they have to be translated into three-dimensional space.

There is also the question of teaching the interface. The first minutes in VR matter especially because the user does not yet know what an interactive object looks like, how far they can reach, or which gestures are recognized. A short, safe introduction reduces errors better than a long block of written instructions.

Progressive disclosure helps preserve attention. Teach one grabbing method first, then a menu, then more complex actions. If everything appears at once, users remember less and are more likely to blame themselves for mistakes even when the design is the real problem.

A good VR interface does not try to demonstrate every capability of the device. It hides technical complexity until the user actually needs it.

The interface should also respect gaze direction. The user should not be forced to search constantly for important elements hidden behind them or placed too high. If something essential is outside the field of view, the environment should provide a gentle cue: sound, movement, light, or another spatial hint. This preserves freedom to look around without abandoning the user.

Good interfaces are tested through observation. If a user spends a long time searching for an object, repeats a gesture, or asks what to do, those are data about the design. Explaining the mistake afterward can help, but changing the environment so the next person understands without explanation is even better. In VR, user behavior becomes one of the main testing tools.

Interface testing should include newcomers. An experienced developer already knows all the conventions and reads the scene differently without realizing it. Someone wearing a headset for the first time reveals which cues truly work. Watching the first few minutes can therefore be more informative than many internal team discussions.

A spatial interface works well when a person quickly transfers rules from one action to another. If, after one successful grab, they already understand how to pick up another object, the system has taught its own language. That is the sign of consistent design: fewer instructions, fewer exceptions, more predictability.

PORTRAIT: DON NORMAN (1935–)

Cognitive scientist and designer Don Norman does not work on VR in the narrow sense, but his ideas about understandable actions, feedback, and matching interfaces to human expectations are especially useful here. If users keep making the same mistake, the problem is often not the user but a device that communicates its possibilities poorly.

PLOT TWIST: A VIRTUAL BUTTON DOES NOT PUSH BACK

Vision says that the finger has touched a panel, while the skin feels no surface. Developers therefore combine visual, auditory, and vibrational feedback in an attempt to bridge the gap between what is seen and what is physically felt.

KEY TERMS

Interaction design – the design of user actions and system responses.

Affordance – a property or cue that suggests what can be done with an object.

Feedback – a system response that confirms or explains an action.

Hand tracking – tracking of hands and fingers without requiring a controller.

Gaze interaction – interaction that uses the direction of the user's gaze.

Haptics – tactile feedback, such as vibration.

Spatial interface – controls and interface elements placed in a three-dimensional environment.

TEST

Choose one correct answer.

1. What does interaction design study and shape?

a) Only texture color

b) Only internet speed

c) The history of computers

d) The relationship between user actions and system responses

2. Why can a virtual door be confusing?

a) Familiar physical cues may be missing

b) Doors cannot be modeled

c) A headset cannot display lines

d) The user cannot perceive depth

3. What is a strength of a controller?

a) It requires no learning at all

b) Physical buttons and precise input

c) It provides the resistance of every virtual object

d) It works without tracking

. . .

4. Why is gaze risky as the only confirmation method?

a) Eyes do not move

b) Gaze cannot be measured

c) People often look without intending to select

d) Gaze always causes nausea

5. Why is feedback necessary?

a) To reduce FOV

b) To turn off sound

c) To increase polygon count

d) To show that the action has been registered

6. Which is an example of haptics?

a) Controller vibration

b) Wall color

c) Stereoscopy

d) A shadow

7. Why can a monitor menu not simply be copied into VR?

a) VR cannot display text

b) There is no fixed screen frame, and viewing distance changes

c) Menus are prohibited

d) The user keeps their eyes closed

8. How can VR direct attention?

a) Only by locking the user's head

b) Only with text

c) With light, sound, and movement

d) It cannot

9. What does affordance mean?

a) Frame rate

b) A type of lens

c) A payment system

d) A cue about a possible action

10. Where does the topic of interaction lead next?

a) To the question of the virtual body and avatar

b) To the history of panoramas

c) To batteries

d) To printing stereoscopic cards

HOME EXPERIMENT

- Choose a cup, a door, or a light switch. Write down the visual and tactile cues that tell you how to use it. Now imagine there is no weight or physical resistance. What feedback would have to be added? In your project, describe three user actions and the world's response to each one.
- *In Lesson 8, hands and controls lead us to a stranger question: what happens when a virtual body starts to feel like your own?*

LESSON 8. WHO ARE YOU INSIDE A VIRTUAL WORLD?

AN AVATAR BEGINS WITH A POINT OF VIEW

You can enter VR without a visible body and see only the scene. But add virtual hands that move with your real hands and the experience changes. They occupy the place where the brain expects the body to continue.

When vision, movement, and touch are sufficiently coordinated, a person can develop a sense of ownership over a virtual limb or body. This does not mean losing awareness of the real body. It reflects the way the brain combines sensory signals into its current model of the self.

THE OLD RUBBER HAND ILLUSION

Research on bodily perception has shown that the sense of hand ownership can be altered. In the classic rubber hand illusion, a rubber hand is placed in view while the participant's real hand is hidden, and both are stimulated in synchrony. Under the right conditions, the person begins to experience the rubber hand as partly connected to their own body.

VR makes such manipulations far more flexible: a virtual hand can be changed in size, position, appearance, and the timing of its movement.

AGENCY AND OWNERSHIP

Sense of agency means the experience that "I caused this action." Sense of ownership means "this body, or this part of it, belongs to me." The two often occur together, but they can come apart.

If a virtual hand follows your real hand accurately, agency is usually strong. If it begins moving on its own, the connection breaks. Such disruptions help researchers study how bodily self-perception is constructed.

SOCIAL PRESENCE

An avatar represents more than one's own body. In multiplayer VR, we see representations of other people. Head turns, gestures, distance, and gaze direction contribute to the feeling of being together in the same place.

Even a simplified avatar can carry social signals if its movements are well linked to the person behind it. Greater visual realism raises expectations: odd facial animation or delayed movement becomes more noticeable.

WHO IS RESPONSIBLE FOR AN AVATAR'S ACTIONS?

When a digital body is closely tied to a person, questions of personal space, moderation, and movement data appear. What counts as an intrusion? How should a system respond to unwanted proximity or gestures? Which data does a service truly need?

We will return to these questions through privacy in Lesson 11. For now, the main point is enough: VR turns the interface from a cursor into a body.

HOW THE BRAIN BUILDS THE FEELING "THIS IS MY BODY"

The sense of owning a body feels so immediate that it is easy to assume it is fixed. In fact, the brain continually combines vision, touch, joint position, movement, and internal signals. When those sources agree, a stable body model emerges. Experiments with bodily illusions show that this model is flexible enough to incorporate unusual combinations of sensory information.

VR demonstrates that flexibility especially clearly. A user sees a virtual hand where they expect their own and watches it move in synchrony with the real hand. Even when its appearance differs, matching movement creates a strong connection. Add noticeable delay or make the hand move in another direction and the feeling quickly weakens. The central principle of the course appears again: consistency matters more than decorative realism.

It is useful to distinguish body ownership from agency because they answer different questions. A person can feel that a virtual hand belongs to them while not fully controlling it. Or they can control an abstract cursor and clearly experience authorship of the action without feeling that the cursor is part of the body. VR allows researchers to separate these components experimentally and observe what happens.

A virtual body can have a different height, proportions, or appearance. Researchers study how such changes affect judgments of distance, behavior, and social situations. These findings should not be turned into simple promises such as "changing your avatar changes your personality." Effects depend on context, task, and experimental design. Still, the ability to alter bodily perspective under controlled conditions makes VR an unusual research tool.

Social presence requires more than two avatars simply being visible. Another person feels more convincing when head turns, gestures, facial movements, and direction of attention arrive at the right time. Even a few well-tracked signals can create the sense of a live conversational partner. By contrast, a highly realistic face with delayed expression can feel stranger than a simple stylized character.

Motion capture transfers bodily movement to a digital model. In ordinary home VR, the system may know only the positions of the head and hands, so elbows, shoulders, and legs have to be estimated algorithmically. Full studio systems use additional markers, cameras, or inertial sensors. More measurement points can produce a more accurate avatar, but they also make the system more complex and expensive.

Virtual bodies have practical uses. In rehabilitation, they can provide visual feedback about movement. In research, they make it possible to alter bodily parameters without physically changing the person. In training, they can demonstrate hand position. In every case, however, evidence still matters: a convincing bodily illusion does not by itself prove medical or educational benefit.

Ethical questions appear too. If a person experiences an avatar as their body, unwanted proximity or contact from another avatar may carry more weight than the same event on a conventional screen. Social platforms therefore use personal boundaries, blocking tools, and interaction settings. No physical contact occurs, but the psychological significance can still be real.

Finally, the body is a source of data. Pose, head movement, gestures, gaze, and facial expression are useful for animation and interaction. The same signals can also be valuable for analytics. In Lesson 11, we will examine the other side of embodiment: the better a virtual environment understands the body, the more carefully we need to decide what information is stored and who receives it.

The sense of a virtual body is also linked to spatial scale. If an avatar is too tall or too short, surrounding objects begin to feel different. A door handle appears at an unexpected height, the table is at the wrong level, and even a step can feel altered. Calibrating height and floor level therefore affects more than appearance. It changes the experience of the world.

Mismatch in arm length is especially noticeable. If a virtual hand appears where the real arm could not physically reach, the brain receives a contradiction. Some systems hide parts of the arm or use stylized bodies precisely because an incomplete but coherent model can work better than an almost realistic one full of errors.

In social interaction, gaze and head orientation matter enormously. Even with simple graphics, people can tell whether someone is facing them. Eye tracking can make an avatar more expressive, but it also turns gaze into a measurable stream of data. Improved social presence is therefore directly connected to privacy.

Voice is part of embodiment too. When sound comes from the avatar's head and changes direction as the person moves, the speaker feels located in space. Small mismatches among lip movement, voice, and gesture can feel odd, especially in realistic characters.

In research, an avatar is sometimes deliberately made different from the user. This allows scientists to study how bodily perspective can affect behavior. The results still require caution: an effect observed in one experiment does not mean that any avatar will automatically change a person's beliefs or personality.

The main practical idea is that the body in VR is simultaneously an interface, an object of perception, and a source of data. Its design therefore cannot be left to the 3D artist alone. Tracking, psychology, social design, safety, and privacy all meet here.

A user's own virtual body also affects distance judgments. The hand acts as a natural ruler: objects are seen relative to the palm, elbow, and shoulder. If the avatar does not match movement well, both body ownership and spatial interaction suffer.

In multiplayer environments, the body becomes a social calling card. Posture, gesture speed, and head direction communicate attitude even before words. Tracking, which may seem like a purely technical feature, therefore becomes part of social communication.

An avatar can also support accessibility. A user does not have to reproduce their physical body visually. They may choose a representation that suits the task or the social setting. But a system should distinguish between harmless personalization and deliberate deception where identity matters. Those norms are still developing alongside the platforms themselves.

Virtual bodies also have the problem of missing parts. A home system often tracks the head and hands but does not know the exact positions of elbows, knees, and feet. An algorithm completes the pose using likely anatomy. When the person moves in ordinary ways, the approximation may go unnoticed. In an unusual pose, the avatar can look strange.

This helps explain why stylization can work better than realism. A simplified body tolerates small tracking errors, while a nearly photographic avatar makes every mismatch visible. The higher the visual expectations, the stricter the requirements for tracking and animation.

Personalization matters in social VR as well. An avatar can help a person express themselves while hiding physical characteristics. In casual social settings, that can be liberating. In business or medical contexts, different identity rules may be needed. Context once again determines the requirements.

Embodiment also affects physical safety. A user may see virtual hands while physically holding controllers and forget the actual size of the device, striking something nearby. The boundaries of the real room and the virtual body therefore have to be designed together.

Ultimately, the virtual body reveals how flexible the idea of an interface can be. On an ordinary computer, the interface sits between the person and the program. In VR, part of the interface becomes the representation of the person themselves. That radically changes the psychological cost of errors and the quality of interaction.

A virtual body can also change emotional distance. A character that approaches an avatar closely may feel more intrusive than the same character on a monitor. Social scenarios should therefore respect familiar zones of personal space and give users control over distance.

The ability to step back quickly, hide another user, change audio volume, or enable a personal boundary can be extremely useful. These functions belong to embodiment too: they protect not the physical body, but the person's experienced digital extension.

This is where it becomes clear that VR cannot be treated as a graphics technology alone. It works with how people locate themselves, their bodies, and other people. Psychological accuracy can therefore matter more than visual accuracy.

The quality of embodiment also depends on latency. Even a beautiful virtual hand stops feeling like your own if it noticeably lags behind the real one. Body tracking is therefore tied to the same milliseconds as head tracking. A virtual body convinces not through appearance alone, but through timely agreement among action, vision, and expected result.

There is a cultural side to avatars as well. A virtual body can be realistic, fantastical, symbolic, or almost absent. The right choice depends on the task and the norms of the community. This course does not declare one style correct. What matters is that the representation of the body supports interaction, does not mislead the user, and fits the context of communication.

The more naturally a virtual body enters into action, the less the user thinks of it as an interface. This is the paradox of embodiment: technically, an avatar consists of a model, tracking, and animation; psychologically, it can be experienced as a temporary extension of the person.

A virtual body also helps measure interaction: the system knows pose, gesture speed, and position relative to objects. These data are useful for animation and analysis, but they require the same rules of minimization and protection that we will return to in the privacy lesson.

PORTRAIT: MEL SLATER

Slater and his colleagues have extensively studied virtual embodiment, social behavior, and body illusions. VR allows researchers to change a body and an environment systematically while keeping experimental conditions under control. It has therefore become not only a medium but also a tool for studying the sense of bodily presence itself.

PLOT TWIST: A VIRTUAL HAND CAN CHANGE A REAL ASSESSMENT OF THREAT

Research on body ownership shows that the degree to which people identify with a virtual body can alter behavior and the perception of risk. An avatar therefore cannot be treated as merely a decorative shell.

KEY TERMS

Avatar – a digital representation of the user.

Embodiment – the experience of having a body and acting through it in VR.

Body ownership – the feeling that a body or body part belongs to you.

Agency – the feeling that you are the author of your own action.

Social presence – the feeling of being together and interacting with other people.

Motion capture – recording movement for transfer to a digital model.

Synchrony – temporal agreement between a real action and its virtual response.

TEST

Choose one correct answer.

1. What is an avatar?

a) A digital representation of the user

b) A type of lens

c) A rotation sensor

d) A physical controller

2. What does body ownership mean?

a) Legal ownership of a headset

b) Movement speed

c) The feeling that a body or body part belongs to you

d) Camera control

3. What is agency?

a) The number of avatars

b) Frame rate

c) Scene depth

d) The feeling of authorship over one's own action

. . .

4. What does the rubber hand illusion show?

a) The sense of the body cannot be altered

b) Body ownership depends on the integration of sensory signals

c) Vision has no influence on body perception

d) VR necessarily causes pain

5. Why is synchrony important?

a) It links visible movement to the user's action

b) It changes color

c) It increases FOV

d) It replaces sound

6. What is social presence?

a) A friends list

b) The internet

c) The feeling of interacting with other people as though they are nearby

d) The number of characters

7. What does motion capture do?

a) Compresses textures

b) Measures temperature

c) Creates lenses

d) Records movement for a digital model

8. Why is a realistic avatar more difficult to create convincingly?

a) It requires smell

b) Errors in facial expression and movement become more noticeable

c) It cannot move

d) It cannot support sound

9. Which issue appears when the interface becomes a digital body?

a) Personal-space boundaries and movement data

b) Resolution alone

c) The history of photography

d) Optics

10. Why is an avatar more than decoration?

a) It is visible only to other people

b) It has no effect on experience

c) It participates in bodily and social perception

d) It is needed only for games

HOME EXPERIMENT

- Stand in front of a mirror and make three gestures: point, shrug, and step back. Which parts of their meaning would disappear if an avatar transmitted only the position of the hands? In your project, decide whether the user sees hands, a full avatar, a tool, or some other representation, and explain why.
- *In Lesson 9, we will leave the perception laboratory and look at the practical problems virtual environments already solve.*

LESSON 9. WHY DO SURGEONS, PILOTS, AND ENGINEERS NEED WORLDS THAT DO NOT EXIST?

TRAINING WHERE MISTAKES COST TOO MUCH

A simulator is valuable not because it resembles a game, but because it allows a situation to be repeated without paying the full price of a real mistake. Aviation has used simulators for decades, and VR extends that logic into other fields. People can rehearse procedures, spatial work, and interaction with equipment.

A simulation is useful only when transfer to the real task has been tested. An impressive virtual scene by itself does not prove that training is effective.

MEDICINE: FROM ANATOMY TO THERAPY

VR is used to teach medical procedures, support rehabilitation, and provide some forms of psychological treatment. Exposure therapy for phobias is especially well known: frightening situations can be presented gradually and under controlled conditions. Researchers have also studied VR for pain and motor rehabilitation.

Caution is essential here. Saying "VR helps" does not mean the technology replaces a clinician or works equally well for every condition. Medical applications are evaluated for specific protocols, patient groups, and measurable outcomes.

A PROJECT BEFORE CONSTRUCTION

An architect or engineer can enter a digital model before the physical version exists. At human scale, it becomes easier to notice an awkward passage, poor visibility, equipment conflicts, or an ergonomic mistake.

Industrial VR often combines CAD models, staff training, and collaborative design review. The benefit appears where spatial perception genuinely matters.

SCIENCE GETS A CONTROLLABLE REALITY

For researchers, VR is unusual because it can create a complex, almost everyday situation while keeping its parameters under experimental control. Distance between people, avatar appearance, height, lighting, and a character's gaze direction can all be changed deliberately.

This makes VR useful for studying perception, social interaction, and movement. But results from a virtual laboratory cannot automatically be generalized to every real-world situation. Ecological validity has to be tested too.

THE MAIN QUESTION: WHAT EXACTLY IMPROVES?

When you hear about a successful VR project, do not ask only, "Did it look impressive?" Ask, "What did they measure?" Time to complete a task? Number of errors? Skill retention a week later? Reduced symptoms? Transfer to real work?

That question guards against a common marketing shortcut. VR is a tool; using it is not, by itself, evidence of benefit.

HOW TO TELL A USEFUL SIMULATION FROM AN EXPENSIVE DEMONSTRATION

VR is especially compelling when people have to act in space. Precisely because it looks impressive, however, the technology can create a false sense of usefulness. A virtual operating room or aircraft cockpit may be striking to see, but the scientific question is different: after this training, does the person perform the real task better, faster, or more safely?

In aviation, the value of simulation has long been established, yet even there a simulator does not replace every form of real practice. It allows rare emergency situations, procedures, crew coordination, and instrument work to be repeated. One of simulation's strengths is repeatability: an instructor can run the same scenario again and again and alter one condition at a time.

Medical tasks differ even more. Learning anatomy depends on spatial structure. Surgical skill depends on motor control, sequence, and feedback. Phobia treatment depends on controlled exposure. It therefore makes little sense to speak of "VR in medicine" as though it were one method. Each application needs its own evidence of effectiveness and safety.

Exposure therapy shows a particular advantage of virtual environments. A real situation may be difficult to arrange, expensive to repeat, or hard to dose precisely. In VR, a therapist can gradually change height, the number of people present, the distance to a feared object, or other parameters. The technology does not replace the clinical logic of treatment. Without an appropriate protocol, the headset remains only a way to present a stimulus.

In rehabilitation, VR can provide immediate visual feedback, turn repetitive exercises into goal-directed tasks, and record movement precisely. But "the exercises were more engaging" is not the same claim as "function recovered better." A study has to define the relevant outcome in advance: range of motion, speed, accuracy, independence in daily life, or another measure.

Engineering and architectural applications use a different advantage: a person can experience a project at the scale of their own body. On an ordinary monitor, it is easy to miss that a passage is too narrow, a control is too high, or a structure blocks the view. VR allows a team to walk through a digital design before fixing the same problem requires an expensive physical rebuild.

Here too, a virtual model is not magical proof that a design is correct. Real materials have weight, resistance, acoustics, temperature, and other properties that a digital model can reproduce only partly. VR is therefore strongest as one stage of design rather than a universal replacement for prototypes and real-world testing.

Research gains experimental control over complex environments. In an ordinary room, it can be difficult to ensure that every participant sees exactly the same event except for one altered variable. In VR, distance, an avatar's facial expression, approach speed, lighting, and many other details can be controlled. This increases experimental control, while also raising the question of whether results transfer to the real world.

A simple four-question filter is useful. What real task is being modeled? Which properties of that task are reproduced and which are not? What outcome is measured? Was it compared with another form of training or treatment? If the answers are vague, the project is probably demonstrating a technology rather than demonstrating an advantage. This filter is useful not only for VR but for almost any new educational or medical technology.

When evaluating a simulator, it helps to distinguish fidelity from validity. Fidelity describes how closely the simulation resembles the real environment in appearance and behavior. Validity asks the more important question: does it actually train what it is supposed to train? High visual fidelity is sometimes essential, for example when a skill depends on exact instrument placement. In other cases, it only raises the cost.

The developer of a training simulation therefore begins with task analysis. What decisions does the professional make? Which mistakes are dangerous? Which signals are critical? What can be repeated without risk? Only then should the team choose the level of graphics and the equipment. Otherwise, the technology starts dictating the content instead of serving it.

Medicine also has a regulatory boundary. An application for general student education and a system claiming a therapeutic effect carry different levels of responsibility. The stronger the medical claim, the stronger the evidence needed for effectiveness, safety, and conditions of use.

Industrial VR is often useful because it gives access to a rare or expensive environment. An employee can learn a sequence of actions on equipment that cannot be shut down for every new trainee. Physical practice is still needed afterward to learn the real machine's weight, resistance, and other physical properties.

Scientific VR has its own trap: the experimenter can control almost everything, but participants know they are in an unusual setup. Researchers therefore compare behavior in virtual and physical conditions to see which conclusions transfer. Control and realism have to be balanced.

A successful simulator may look modest beside an advertising video. It may rehearse one procedure, contain few objects, and have no open world. If that narrow scene reduces errors and speeds learning, it is more valuable than an enormous but purposeless virtual universe.

Simulation has another strength: it can record the process. The system can save the sequence of actions, reaction times, hand trajectories, and errors. An instructor gains material for review, and a learner can repeat a difficult moment. Such analytics are useful only when the metrics are genuinely related to quality of performance.

Detailed recording immediately brings us back to privacy. In a corporate simulator, error data may be used for instruction or for employee evaluation. Those are not the same purpose and they require different rules of access. A technological tool quickly becomes an organizational one.

A mature VR system therefore describes not only the virtual scene but its context of use: who is training, who is evaluating, what data are stored, and when virtual skill is tested in the real task.

Virtual training is especially useful for rare events. A real emergency cannot be created every day for practice, while a simulator can reproduce it repeatedly. Repetition should still be combined with variation. Otherwise, the learner may memorize one staged sequence rather than understand the general principle.

A good simulation therefore contains variations. The location of the fault changes, the order of signals changes, or the timing of an event changes. The learner has to recognize the situation and make a decision rather than remember where the correct tool was placed last time.

There is also a cost to excessive realism. If a team spends months reproducing decorative details exactly but fails to model the causal structure of the task, learning will not improve. The right fidelity applies first to the elements that actually determine the skill.

VR can also make the invisible visible: highlight a hazard zone, show airflow, display a force vector, or reveal the inside of a mechanism. This is a deliberate departure from reality that can improve understanding. The simulation becomes an explanation rather than a copy.

The practical value of VR therefore often appears where the real environment is too dangerous, expensive, rare, invisible, or difficult to control for training. Those constraints should be stated before choosing the technology.

Professional simulators also raise the question of the instructor. VR can record errors automatically, but it cannot always explain what those errors mean. An experienced professional sees the context: why the learner chose an action, what they failed to notice, and which skill needs more work.

The best systems therefore often combine automatic analytics with human review. The technology makes a rare situation repeatable and measurable; the instructor turns the data into learning.

VR is strongest as a tool for extending practice rather than as an autonomous replacement for expertise. It provides a safe scene, while the purpose of the exercise still comes from the task and the teaching method.

A practical project should define in advance what happens after the virtual training. If the skill cannot be checked outside the simulation, its real value is hard to judge. Professional programs therefore often end with an observed task, an examination, or practice on real equipment. VR becomes an intermediate safe step rather than the final destination of training.

A simulator also needs to acknowledge the limits of its model. If a virtual tool does not reproduce weight, that matters when the skill is assessed. If physical force is critical, another simulator or real practice is required. Honest description of what a simulation does not reproduce makes it more useful and protects against inflated expectations.

The success of a simulation is therefore measured not by time spent in the headset, but by changes in behavior outside it. The more precisely the real skill and the method of testing it are defined, the easier it becomes to decide whether VR is justified.

A good professional VR project begins not with a list of headset capabilities, but with a map of the real activity. Only after we understand where people make mistakes, what is dangerous to repeat, and which skills are difficult to teach by ordinary means can we decide whether a virtual environment belongs there.

PORTRAIT: BARBARA ROTHBAUM

American clinical psychologist Barbara Rothbaum was among the researchers who developed and studied virtual-reality exposure therapy for anxiety disorders and post-traumatic stress disorder (PTSD). Her work is a useful example of VR moving from engineering demonstrations into clinical research, where the technology must meet standards of evidence and safety.

PLOT TWIST: SOMETIMES A VIRTUAL COPY IS VALUABLE BECAUSE IT DOES NOT COPY REALITY LITERALLY

A simulation can pause a process, repeat a rare accident, remove unnecessary risk, change scale, or make the invisible visible. The goal is often not a perfect copy of the world, but a way to isolate the skill that matters.

KEY TERMS

Simulator – an environment that reproduces the essential properties of a real task.

Skill transfer – the application of learned behavior in another, usually real-world, situation.

Exposure therapy – gradual, controlled confrontation with feared stimuli.

Rehabilitation – restoration of function and skills after illness or injury.

CAD – computer-aided design and digital engineering models.

Ecological validity – the extent to which behavior in an experiment corresponds to behavior in a real-world context.

Outcome – a measurable result of an intervention or training process.

TEST

Choose one correct answer.

1. Why is a simulator useful for dangerous tasks?

a) It makes all future mistakes impossible

b) It allows the situation to be repeated without paying the full cost of a real mistake

c) It is always more accurate than reality

d) It requires no instruction

2. What needs to be demonstrated for training in VR?

a) Only beautiful graphics

b) A long session

c) A high price

d) Skill transfer or another measurable outcome

3. How can VR be used for some phobias?

a) For controlled exposure

b) To erase memories

c) To diagnose a person from gaze alone

d) As a mandatory replacement for therapy

4. What can VR give an engineer before construction?

a) A guarantee that there are no errors

b) A free physical model

c) A chance to evaluate the space at human scale

d) Automatic project approval

5. Why is VR useful to a researcher?

a) It eliminates the need for an experiment

b) It allows control over parameters in a complex environment

c) It displays thoughts directly

d) It always reproduces reality perfectly

6. What is skill transfer?

a) Copying a file

b) Changing an avatar

c) Moving a controller

d) Applying what was learned in another situation

7. What does CAD refer to?

a) Computer-aided design

b) A type of sound

c) A diagnosis

d) A type of cybersickness

. . .

8. What should you ask when evaluating effectiveness?

a) What logo was used?

b) How much advertising was there?

c) What outcome was measured?

d) What color was the headset?

9. Why is an exact copy of reality not always necessary?

a) Copies are impossible

b) A simulation can emphasize the skill that matters

c) VR cannot support geometry

d) Reality has no rules

10. What is one limitation of VR research?

a) Behavior cannot be measured

b) Conditions cannot be changed

c) Avatars cannot be used

d) Results cannot automatically be generalized to every real-world situation

HOME EXPERIMENT

- Choose a skill that would be dangerous, expensive, or difficult to train in the real world. Make two lists: what a simulation would need to reproduce accurately, and what could be simplified. In your project, define one measurable outcome: what will the user learn or be able to do after the experience?
- *In Lesson 10, we will examine one of VR's most attractive promises: does "being inside the subject" actually help people learn better?*

LESSON 10. CAN YOU LEARN WHAT A CLASSROOM CANNOT SHOW YOU?

MAKING THE INVISIBLE VISIBLE

Education is drawn to VR because scale can be changed at will. A molecule can be enlarged to the size of a room, the Solar System can be shrunk, a historical space can be reconstructed, and a complex mechanism can be taken apart around the learner. A spatial model is useful when something is difficult to imagine from a two-dimensional diagram.

But spectacle is not the same as understanding. A learner can remember the experience and miss the principle.

ACTIVITY HAS TO SERVE THE LEARNING GOAL

Good educational VR connects action to purpose. If the goal is to understand the structure of the heart, it may help to follow blood flow and identify relationships among parts. If the goal is to master a procedure, the learner needs to make decisions and receive feedback.

Collecting virtual objects does not become learning simply because it happens inside a headset.

COGNITIVE LOAD

VR presents many signals at once: space, sound, controls, and bodily movement. This can help, but it can also overload working memory. A beginner may spend attention on operating the system instead of understanding the content.

The interface of an educational environment should therefore be especially simple. The more difficult the subject, the fewer unnecessary actions should be imposed on the learner.

WHERE VR HAS A GENUINE ADVANTAGE

The strongest cases are those in which space or action is part of the knowledge itself: anatomy, safety training, equipment operation, navigation, and some laboratory or social scenarios.

If a book, video, or ordinary model already solves the learning problem well, VR may be an expensive decoration. The technology is justified by its fit with the task, not by novelty.

HOW TO TEST LEARNING

Immediately after a lesson, students may love an impressive new technology. The stricter questions are different: what do they remember later, can they apply the knowledge, do they make fewer errors, and do they understand the principle better than a comparison group?

In education, engagement is easily confused with outcome. They may be related, but one does not guarantee the other.

WHY THE WOW FACTOR CAN DISTORT EVALUATION

A new technology almost inevitably captures attention during the first few minutes. The headset itself is novel; so is the ability to look around, pick up a virtual object, or change scale. This may increase motivation. But a researcher needs to separate novelty of the interface from long-term learning. If a week later the learner remembers only that "it looked amazing," the educational goal was poorly served.

Cognitive theories of multimedia learning remind us that working memory is limited. A user must understand the subject while learning the controls, monitoring the surrounding space, and keeping track of the task. Every extra element competes for attention. In VR, that competition can be especially strong because the environment surrounds the learner and offers many possible directions to look.

Good educational experiences therefore often begin by limiting freedom. This does not mean locking the user rigidly in place. It means giving the experience a clear sequence. First, the user learns one action. Then they receive a task in which that action supports the learning principle. Only after that is secure are new elements added. This may look less impressive in a promotional video, but it can support learning more effectively.

VR's spatial advantage is most obvious when the knowledge itself has a three-dimensional structure. Anatomical relationships among organs, the arrangement of engine parts, a safe route through an industrial space, or molecular geometry can genuinely benefit from changing viewpoint. But if the task is simply to memorize a list of terms, a headset may offer nothing that flash cards cannot.

Activity matters too. Merely looking at a virtual model is not always enough. An action connected to a question is stronger: find a fault in a mechanism, trace a flow, assemble a structure and see what follows from a wrong step, predict an outcome and then test it. In such tasks, the virtual environment becomes a laboratory rather than scenery.

The difficulty of the controls should remain lower than the difficulty of the subject. If a learner spends a long time figuring out how to grab an object, teleport, and open menus, attention is being spent on the interface rather than the lesson. Educational applications often benefit from simple controls, large targets, clear prompts, and instructions that can be repeated. A good interface becomes almost invisible.

Engagement has value, but it should be measured separately. A learner may become more interested in the subject and return to practice more often. That is useful in its own right. It should not, however, be used as a substitute for knowledge or skill. Research needs to distinguish enjoyment, presence, memory, understanding, and transfer to a new situation.

Claims that "VR teaches better" require especially careful comparisons. Better than what? A conventional lecture, a well-made video, hands-on practice, a tabletop model, or a desktop simulation? If the comparison condition is weak, the new technology's advantage can easily be exaggerated. A fair comparison gives the alternative group a high-quality method, not an intentionally dull substitute.

There is an economic question too. Even if VR produces a modest learning gain, the cost of equipment, support, setup time, physical space, teacher training, and software updates still matters. In a school or university, usefulness is determined not only by an effect in a laboratory study, but by whether the technology can be used reliably in practice.

The mature question is therefore not "Does education need VR?" but "For which specific learning goal is VR more suitable than other tools?" This frees us from having to be either enthusiasts or opponents of the technology. Sometimes the answer will be a confident yes, sometimes no, and sometimes "there is not enough evidence yet." That is the scientific way to discuss a new educational medium.

Educational design improves when the learner understands the goal before putting on the headset. If a person first has to learn the controls, then search for the right object, and only at the end remember the subject of the lesson, the technology has consumed its own benefit. Part of the introductory instruction is therefore often better delivered outside VR.

Segmentation is useful too. A complex scene can be revealed gradually: first the main parts, then the relationships, then a task. In the physical world, you cannot remove unnecessary organs from a body or pause a machine halfway through a process. In a virtual environment, you can. Controlled simplification is often the real educational advantage.

Feedback matters. A message that simply says "wrong" teaches little. It is better to show which action led to the error or let the learner repeat the step. In procedural training, the connection between an error and its consequences can be especially valuable when those consequences can be shown safely and without unnecessary dramatization.

Collaborative learning creates another scenario. Several learners can inhabit the same virtual model, discuss an object, and point to parts of the space. Social interaction, however, increases interface complexity and requires communication rules. Multiplayer should be added only when collaboration serves the learning goal.

Access to hardware matters too. One headset for an entire class requires a different method from a headset for every learner. Sometimes VR is best used as a short practice station while the rest of the lesson relies on discussion and ordinary materials. The technology does not have to occupy the whole learning process.

A simple test of mature educational VR is this: if you remove the word "virtual," is there still a clear pedagogical task? If not, the project is probably built around the gadget. If there is, then you can ask whether a spatial environment offers a better way to solve that task.

VR can be particularly useful for repetition because the same scene can be restarted without consuming materials or preparing a physical laboratory. Repetition alone, however, does not guarantee learning. If the learner performs the same action mechanically each time, they may learn to complete the scenario without understanding the principle.

Tasks should therefore vary conditions and require transfer. After one situation has been mastered, change the object's position, the order of actions, or the starting parameters. If the knowledge is genuine, the learner will cope with more than a memorized sequence.

This is one area where virtual environments are especially powerful: parameters can be changed in software. A good course uses that flexibility not for randomness, but to test understanding. Learning begins when a person can explain and apply a rule beyond one attractive scenario.

There is also the problem of context transfer. A learner may perform perfectly in a virtual laboratory and then struggle beside real equipment because of weight, resistance, and noise. Educational design therefore needs to plan a bridge between virtual and physical practice.

Sometimes that bridge is built through a mixed sequence: explanation, VR practice, work with a real object, and then review of errors. The virtual environment occupies the part of the process where it is strongest instead of trying to replace the entire process.

Educational VR is also useful for mistakes that would be too expensive in reality. A learner can assemble a mechanism incorrectly and see the consequences without damaging equipment. Those consequences should be pedagogically clear, not merely dramatic.

Technical familiarity has to be considered. If some students already know VR while others are putting on a headset for the first time, results may reflect differences in interface experience rather than understanding of the subject. Research and teaching practice need to control for this factor.

A strong educational environment is therefore usually transparent about its purpose. The learner knows what they are studying, which action matters, and how understanding will be tested. The headset is a means, not the content of the lesson.

Educational VR is also worth evaluating with a delayed test. Immediately after a vivid session, scores may be high because attention was intense and the experience is fresh. Several days later, we can see whether understanding remains and whether the learner can apply it without the headset.

A good course also checks explanations, not only correct answers. If a learner can state the principle in their own words and apply it in another problem, that is stronger evidence of learning than successful repetition of a virtual scenario.

VR is therefore especially interesting as a medium for practice and visualization, but it does not cancel the old educational questions: what did the learner understand, what did they remember, and what can they now do independently?

The teacher or course designer also needs a way to see where the learner went wrong. A score alone is not enough. A log of the action sequence, a replay of a key moment, or a visual marker of the problematic step may be more useful. VR then produces material for discussion rather than an isolated personal experience that is difficult to connect with the rest of the course.

The technology can also support individual pacing: a learner can repeat a difficult stage as many times as needed instead of waiting for access to rare equipment. Personalization is useful only when the goal remains clear. Unlimited freedom to repeat a scene without feedback can easily become entertainment instead of deliberate practice.

The best educational scenario leaves behind knowledge that works without the headset. If a learner can explain the principle, recognize a new situation, and apply a skill in another context, VR has done its job.

That criterion protects education from technological fashion. If understanding, skill, and the ability to reason remain after the headset comes off, the environment worked. If only the memory of an unusual interface remains, the pedagogical problem is still unsolved.

In that sense, the best educational interface is unobtrusive: attention stays on the subject, while the technology provides a space for action, testing, and repetition.

PORTRAIT: RICHARD MAYER

Psychologist Richard Mayer is known for his research on multimedia learning. His work is not specifically about VR, but it provides a useful framework: educational material has to respect the limits of attention and working memory. A new technology is effective when it helps learners process relevant information, not when it merely adds more stimulation.

PLOT TWIST: SOMETIMES THE LESS SPECTACULAR VERSION TEACHES BETTER

Decorative animation, complicated controls, and unnecessary objects can consume attention and leave a learner with a weaker understanding of the subject. In educational VR, simplification can sometimes be an advantage rather than a flaw.

KEY TERMS

Cognitive load – the amount of mental resources a task requires.

Working memory – a system for temporarily holding and processing a limited amount of information.

Learning objective – a specific result the learner should understand or be able to perform.

Feedback – information about the result of an action or answer.

Learning transfer – the ability to apply what was learned in a new situation.

Engagement – the degree of a person's attention and participation.

Control group – a comparison group in a study.

TEST

Choose one correct answer.

1. Which advantage of VR is especially clear in education?

a) Working with spatial or otherwise hard-to-access objects

b) Eliminating the teacher

c) Automatically memorizing any information

d) Guaranteeing a high grade

2. Why is spectacle not the same as learning?

a) Beautiful scenes are always harmful

b) A memorable experience may not produce understanding

c) Learning does not use vision

d) VR prevents explanation

3. What is cognitive load?

a) The weight of the headset

b) Network speed

c) File size

d) The mental demands of a task

4. Why can VR be harder for a beginner?

a) Some attention is spent on learning the controls

b) Beginners cannot see in 3D

c) VR is only for experts

d) Beginners cannot hear sound

5. When is VR especially appropriate?

a) Always

b) Only in games

c) When space or action is part of the knowledge

d) Only when there are no books

6. What is learning transfer?

a) Applying knowledge in a new situation

b) Copying a lesson

c) Changing classrooms

d) Handing the headset to another person

7. Why is a control group useful?

a) To increase FOV

b) To compare the effect of an intervention

c) To record sound

d) To adjust the lenses

8. What matters more than a rating of "I liked it"?

a) Device price

b) Number of visual effects

c) Session length

d) Testing whether knowledge is retained and can be applied

9. Why can simplification help?

a) It always makes the facts themselves easier

b) It increases resolution

c) It reduces distracting cognitive load

d) It replaces practice

10. Where does the discussion of learning effects lead next?

a) To the history of the stereoscope

b) To questions of data, influence, and responsibility

c) To polygon settings

d) To buying hardware

HOME EXPERIMENT

Choose a topic that is difficult to explain on a flat page. Invent one action in VR that would genuinely help someone understand it. Then remove every decorative element that is not necessary for that action to make sense. In your project, add an educational or practical task and a way to test the result.

In Lesson 11, we will turn to the price of a convincing environment: what data it collects, and why bodily movement can become sensitive information.

LESSON 11. WHAT DOES VIRTUAL REALITY KNOW ABOUT YOU?

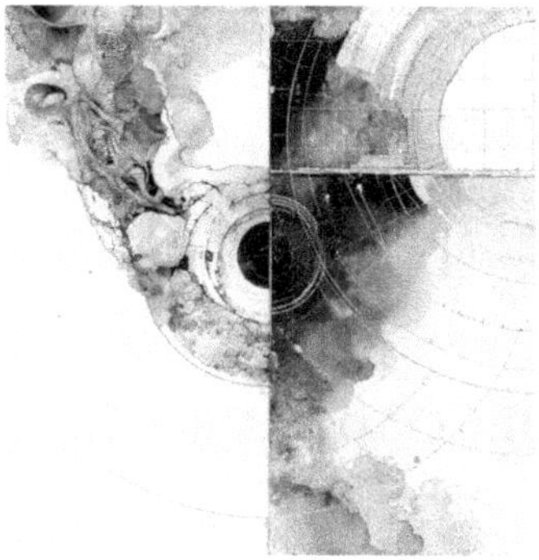

DATA BEGIN WITH THE POSITION OF YOUR HEAD

For VR to work, the system has to measure movement continuously. The positions of the head and hands, and sometimes the eyes and facial movements, become streams of data. Some of this information may be needed only on the device for rendering. But if it is stored, linked to an account, or sent to a service, privacy questions arise.

These data differ from an ordinary click. Patterns of bodily movement can be relatively stable and individual, while gaze can reveal what attracts attention and for how long.

EYE TRACKING: A USEFUL SENSOR AND A SENSITIVE CHANNEL

Eye tracking can be used to select interface elements, improve rendering, and study attention. At the same time, it creates a record of where a person looked. Context matters greatly: the risk is different in a game, a medical application, and a workplace simulator.

It would be wrong to treat every gaze record automatically as a unique biometric identifier, but it would also be wrong to treat gaze as nothing more than a harmless cursor.

THE ROOM BECOMES PART OF THE DATA

Headsets with outward-facing cameras build a representation of the surrounding space so they can track movement and combine digital content with the physical world. The device is therefore working with room geometry and visual information around the user.

Storage architecture, local processing, application permissions, and understandable access settings all matter.

MANIPULATION IN AN ENVIRONMENT THAT COMMANDS ATTENTION

VR can control a large share of the user's visual field and spatial audio. Dark patterns, intrusive advertising, or deliberately confusing interfaces can carry extra force because the person is inside the environment and acts through the body.

Ethics is not an add-on to a finished product. Decisions about what to measure, what to store, and how to direct attention are built into the architecture from the start.

PERSONAL SPACE WITHOUT A PHYSICAL WALL

In social VR, another person's avatar can come too close or make a gesture that feels intrusive. There is no physical contact, but the psychological response can be real. Platforms therefore introduce personal boundaries, blocking, communication controls, and moderation.

A digital space does not become "unreal" merely because it is computed.

WHY MOVEMENT DATA DIFFER FROM ORDINARY WEBSITE ANALYTICS

An ordinary website may record what a user clicked, how long they stayed on a page, and which page or service referred them. VR can work with a much denser stream of bodily information. A headset continually estimates head position. Controllers or cameras track the hands. Some devices also collect gaze direction, facial pose, and information about the surrounding space. All of these signals can support functions the user genuinely wants.

The problem begins not with measurement itself, but with what happens to the data afterward. It is one thing for head coordinates to be processed locally and disappear fractions of a second later. It is another for movements to be logged, linked to an account, analyzed for advertising, or shared with a third party. The same sensor signal carries different risks depending on the information flow.

Eye tracking illustrates the difference well. Foveated rendering needs to know where the user is looking now so that computation can be allocated efficiently. An interface can use gaze as a pointer. A researcher can use it to study attention. An advertising system may be interested in the same data as an indicator of what a person noticed and how long they looked. The technical source is the same; the purpose of processing is not.

Room data present a similar case. Inside-out tracking depends on visual references. Passthrough and mixed reality use cameras to show the physical environment and place digital objects inside it. A geometric representation of walls and furniture may be built for these functions. Privacy architecture therefore needs to answer: what is processed on the device, what leaves it, what is stored, and for how long?

Behavioral biometrics complicate the picture. A person's movements are not necessarily a unique "fingerprint" in every context, but research shows that sets of kinematic features can help distinguish users. Large collections of telemetry therefore should not automatically be treated as anonymous merely because they contain no name or photograph.

Medical and workplace scenarios can be especially sensitive. In a therapeutic application, movement and gaze may indirectly reflect symptoms, fears, or limitations. In a corporate simulator, telemetry may be used to evaluate task performance. Decisions about storage and access then affect the relationship between a patient and a clinic or an employee and an employer.

Data minimization offers a simple principle: collect only what is genuinely needed for the stated function, keep it no longer than necessary, and separate different purposes of processing. If eye position is needed for rendering, that does not automatically create a moral justification for storing gaze history for any future purpose. Technical capability is not permission.

Consent creates another problem. A long user agreement may formally list many kinds of data processing, but a person wearing a headset is rarely in a position to evaluate every sensor stream item by item. Clear settings, reasonable defaults, and the ability to withdraw permission without losing unrelated functions therefore matter. Good privacy design does not turn refusal into a punishment.

Social VR adds data about other people. Voice, gestures, avatars, messages, and behavior in a shared space may all be relevant to moderation. A platform needs to protect users from harassment without turning protection into uncontrolled surveillance. This is no longer a purely engineering problem: safety, privacy, freedom of expression, and community rules intersect.

The question "What does VR know about you?" therefore has two answers. Technically, the system knows what its sensors and interface need in order to function. Organizationally, a service knows what it chooses to store, link, and use. The first level is shaped by the physics of the device, the second by company policy and law. Users encounter both, but responsibility is distributed differently.

Privacy becomes harder because VR data are also high-frequency. A click on a website is a single event; head position may be updated many times per second. Even a short session creates a long time series. That density can support much more detailed behavioral analysis than users intuitively expect.

Aggregation does not always solve the problem completely. Removing a name while retaining a rich movement sequence and other features can leave the data sensitive. Anonymization therefore has to be treated as a technical problem, not as the deletion of one field.

Permission systems should also be meaningful. A request to "allow camera access" tells the user very little about whether images will leave the device, be stored, or be used only for local tracking. Good interfaces explain the purpose and consequences, not merely the name of the sensor.

Secondary use is another issue. Data may have been collected to improve tracking and later become valuable for behavioral research or advertising. Contextual integrity reminds us that a new purpose requires its own justification. Agreement to one function is not unlimited permission for every future function.

For teenagers and educational institutions, the stakes are particularly high. A school may use VR as a learning tool, but that does not make every form of analytics automatically acceptable. Educational necessity, data minimization, and transparency need to be considered separately from a platform's commercial interests.

Privacy does not mean complete secrecy. A user may willingly share an avatar and voice in a social space while never expecting their gaze history or hand kinematics to be stored indefinitely. The boundary depends on context and expectations, not on a simple rule that "everything is public" or "everything is private."

VR privacy also concerns people around the user. A headset camera can see the room and incidentally capture people who never agreed to participate in a digital service. Local processing and restricted access to raw imagery therefore matter even for people who never put on the headset.

Data security is different from privacy. A company may have a legitimate and clearly stated reason to collect data but protect its servers poorly against a breach. Conversely, data can be encrypted well and still be collected in quantities the user does not need. These questions should be asked separately.

A mature system therefore combines minimization, security, understandable settings, and purpose limitation. One checkbox that says "I agree" is not enough if the architecture was designed around excessive observation from the beginning.

VR data can be useful to users themselves. Movement history can show progress in rehabilitation, a coach can demonstrate changes in technique, and a developer can discover an awkward interface. The problem is not analytics as such, but whether purpose, access, and retention are transparent.

Separation is a useful design principle: data for an immediate function, data for product diagnostics, and data for profiling should not automatically flow into one undifferentiated pool. The clearer the architecture, the easier it is to explain what is happening to the user.

In social spaces, privacy intersects with safety. A platform may need event logs to investigate complaints, but continuous recording of all behavior creates new risks. The solution requires proportionality: collect enough to protect people without turning the environment into total surveillance.

Eye tracking is especially sensitive because attention is often involuntary. A person may look at an object from curiosity, fear, or accident. Treating every glance as a preference is dangerous. Data need context, not merely volume.

That is why the privacy policy of a good VR system should already be visible in the design of its features. A legal document written at the end cannot repair an architecture that collects more than it needs.

Privacy by design means considering privacy before a product launches. Developers decide in advance which sensors are necessary, where data are processed, how long they are kept, and who has access. This is more reliable than trying to restrict a large body of accumulated data after the fact.

Users also need to be able to understand the system without legal training. If a feature requires eye tracking, the interface should explain why. If movement history is stored to track progress, the user should know how long it is kept and how to delete it.

The more bodily a computing environment becomes, the less acceptable the model of "collect everything just in case" becomes. In VR, data minimization is not only a legal principle. It is part of trust in the technology itself.

Trust also depends on being able to use a basic function without unnecessary profiling. If head tracking is essential to VR, it should work independently of consent to advertising analytics. Separating required data from optional data makes the user's choice real. Otherwise, formal consent becomes a condition of access rather than a meaningful decision.

PORTRAIT: HELEN NISSENBAUM

Philosopher and privacy researcher Helen Nissenbaum developed the concept of contextual integrity. Privacy depends not only on whether data are secret, but also on whether their flow matches the norms of a particular context. This is especially useful for VR: gaze data may be needed for rendering, but that does not answer whether they are also appropriate for advertising or external analytics.

PLOT TWIST: BODY MOVEMENT CAN BE AN IDENTIFYING SIGNAL

- Research shows that behavioral patterns in VR movement can potentially distinguish among users. Practical accuracy depends on the dataset and method, so it would be wrong to claim that any movement always reveals a person’s identity. But the possibility itself changes how we should think about telemetry.

KEY TERMS

Telemetry – data collected automatically about system operation and user actions.

Eye tracking – measurement of gaze direction and eye movement.

Biometric data – data about physical or behavioral characteristics used, under appropriate processing, to recognize a person.

Privacy – norms and control governing how information about a person is handled.

Local processing – processing data on the device without necessarily sending them to an external server.

Dark pattern – a design technique that steers users toward a choice that benefits the service.

Moderation – rules and tools used to manage behavior and content.

TEST

Choose one correct answer.

1. Which data does VR almost inevitably use in order to function?

a) Your tax return

b) The addresses of all your friends

c) Your reading history

d) Head movement

2. Why can eye tracking be sensitive?

a) It always contains a password

b) It measures only eye color

c) It can reveal the direction and duration of attention

d) It is never useful for rendering

3. What can outward-facing cameras observe?

a) The surrounding physical environment

b) Only virtual objects

c) Only the display

d) Only the controller

4. What does local processing mean?

a) Printing the data

b) Processing the data on the device itself

c) Sending the data to any server

d) Removing the sensors

. . .

5. Why can VR interfaces have unusually strong influence?

a) Users cannot think while in VR

b) VR always hypnotizes people

c) Headsets prevent users from leaving

d) They can control a large part of the user's sensory environment

6. What is a dark pattern?

a) A dark texture

b) Night mode

c) Manipulative choice architecture

d) A display fault

7. Why do personal boundaries matter in social VR?

a) Virtual proximity can trigger a real psychological response

b) Avatars have physical weight

c) Everyone is physically standing next to each other

d) The network cannot function without boundaries

8. What does contextual integrity say?

a) All data are equivalent

b) Whether a data flow is appropriate depends on context and norms

c) Privacy is the same thing as a password

d) All data collection is prohibited

9. Can we say that any movement pattern always identifies a person uniquely?

a) Yes, always

b) Only for children

c) Only without a headset

d) No. It depends on the data and the method

10. What final question does the topic of data lead toward?

a) Who invented the stereoscope?

b) How do you make a texture?

c) What changes if VR becomes an ordinary computing environment?

d) How does an accelerometer work?

HOME EXPERIMENT

- Open the permission settings for any app on your phone and look at which data it requests. You do not need to change anything. For your project, write three lines: which data are genuinely necessary, which data should not be collected, and what the user should be able to delete or disable.
- *In Lesson 12, we will bring the course together and try to distinguish real directions of VR development from promises that remain marketing claims or research hypotheses.*

LESSON 12. WHAT HAPPENS IF VIRTUAL WORLDS BECOME AS ORDINARY AS SCREENS?

THE FUTURE OF VR MAY BE LESS VIRTUAL

At the start of the course, it is easy to picture VR as a closed headset that replaces reality. But device development increasingly brings VR, AR, and MR together. Cameras show the physical room, digital windows remain anchored in space, and interfaces respond to hands and gaze.

The result may not be one enormous virtual world, but spatial computers that vary the amount of digital content according to the situation. The boundary between "entering VR" and simply "using a computer" may become less noticeable.

LIGHTNESS MAY MATTER MORE THAN SPECTACULAR PHOTOREALISM

For a technology to become part of everyday life, the device has to be comfortable, safe, socially acceptable, and sufficiently self-contained. Weight, heat, battery life, optics, and the ability to see the physical world quickly may matter just as much as maximum graphical quality.

The history of technology often shows that the mass market is not necessarily won by the most powerful option, but by the one that is good enough and gets in the way of life less.

TOUCH STILL LAGS BEHIND

A virtual object can be seen and heard convincingly, yet the hand still passes through empty air. Vibration helps, and gloves and other haptic systems try to convey touch and resistance, but there is no universal lightweight substitute for physical contact.

Vision and hearing are comparatively easy to stimulate through devices. Force, weight, temperature, and texture require direct physical effects on the body.

A BRAIN-COMPUTER INTERFACE IS NOT A TELEPORTER INTO THE MIND

Brain-computer interfaces often appear in predictions about the future of VR. Current systems can record specific patterns of neural activity and decode them for limited tasks, including communication, device control, and some clinical applications. That is very different from unrestricted access to a person's thoughts, let alone directly delivering a rich virtual world into consciousness.

The more spectacular the prediction, the more carefully we should distinguish a working technology, an experimental prototype, and a promise.

THE METAVERSE: ONE IDEA, NO SINGLE IMPLEMENTATION

The word "metaverse" has been used for persistent multiplayer worlds, social VR platforms, digital-object economies, and interconnected service spaces. There is no single mandatory form of the idea.

It is therefore more useful to examine specific functions: shared presence, continuity of identity, interoperability among services, work, education, and entertainment. Some of these are developing independently of the grand label.

THE CENTRAL PROBLEM IS STILL HUMAN

We have traveled from two images presented to the eyes to digital bodies and questions of privacy. In every case, VR worked well only when the technology accounted for the human being inside it.

The world has to respond to movement in time. The interface has to explain what actions mean. A simulation has to produce measurable benefit for a real task. Data have to be collected for a reason. The future of VR will be shaped not only by computing power, but by the quality of the relationship between system and person.

The question "Will VR become the next computer?" remains open. Some of its technologies may dissolve into everyday devices and stop being called VR. Specialized headsets may remain the best tool for particular tasks. After this course, what matters is not predicting the winner, but knowing how to examine the next promise.

HOW TO TALK ABOUT THE FUTURE WITHOUT BECOMING A PROPHET

A final lesson tempts us to turn the course into a list of predictions. In five years, headsets will look like this; in ten, the metaverse will arrive; after that, brain-computer interfaces will replace controllers. The problem is that the history of VR has already taught us caution. The technology has repeatedly been declared on the verge of a mass-market revolution, while real development moved in waves and along unexpected routes.

It is more reliable to predict engineering pressures than products. Headsets are under pressure to become lighter. Optics must produce wider, sharper images with less thickness. Tracking must work more reliably across different rooms. Input systems are trying to understand hands, eyes, and voice more naturally. Batteries need to last longer, while computation has to generate less heat. These problems exist regardless of which company wins the market.

The blending of VR and AR also looks like a logical direction. If a device can show the physical room through cameras and place digital objects accurately within it, users can choose how immersed they want to be. For a game, the device may hide the real world. For work, it may leave a physical keyboard visible. For communication, it may show another person alongside virtual material. At that point, VR, MR, and spatial computing begin to describe modes of one platform rather than entirely separate technologies.

Touch develops more slowly than vision for a fundamental reason. To display an object, a system only has to control the light reaching the eyes. To reproduce the resistance of a wall, it has to apply force to the hand. Weight requires directed load, texture requires stimulation of the skin, and temperature requires control of heat transfer. A universal lightweight system would have to reproduce many different physical effects without obstructing movement. That is much harder than vibrating a controller.

Brain-computer interfaces require especially careful language. Modern BCIs can measure certain patterns of brain activity and use them in limited tasks, particularly in medical research and assistive technology. This does not imply the ability to read arbitrary thoughts freely or write a rich virtual scene directly into the brain. There is an enormous scientific distance between measuring a signal and achieving "full immersion through the brain."

The metaverse is a useful example of how a marketing term can gather many technologies under one roof. Persistent digital worlds, avatars, social presence, virtual economies, and transferable digital objects all exist in different forms. But there is no single required technical implementation that automatically turns these elements into one metaverse. It is better to analyze the functions separately.

An everyday spatial-computing environment would also face social constraints. People need to understand when someone nearby is recording the room, looking at a virtual screen, or taking part in a remote meeting. Norms will develop, much as they once did around mobile phones and cameras. The technical possibility of wearing a device all day does not mean society is ready to accept it in every situation.

Economics will shape the future too. Even an excellent technology does not become widespread if it is too expensive, difficult to set up, or lacks tasks people value enough. Conversely, a specialized tool can succeed without billions of users. VR for industrial training, therapy, or design does not have to become a universal household headset in order to matter.

There is also the possibility of disappearance through success. Many computing functions stop being perceived as separate technologies once they become ordinary. GPS was once a specialized technical marvel; now users simply expect a map to know where they are. If spatial tracking, 3D interfaces, and digital objects become ordinary parts of computing, the term VR may be used less often even while its ideas are everywhere.

The best outcome of this course is therefore not a forecast but a method of evaluation. When a new headset or a grand promise appears, ask five questions. Which human signal does the system measure? How quickly and accurately does it respond? Which real task does it solve better than existing tools? What new data and risks does it create? What has already been demonstrated, and what remains a prototype, demonstration, or plan? These questions will outlive particular device models.

In Lesson 1, we asked whether the brain can be made to believe in another world. We can now answer more precisely. It is possible to build a sensory and interactive environment coherent enough that a person experiences presence and acts within it through the body. But the technology does not erase reality. It builds a new layer of experience on top of human perception. The more convincing that layer becomes, the more important it is to understand not only how it works, but why it is needed.

The future of VR will also depend on standards. If applications are tied to one device and cannot share common methods for tracking and input, development costs rise and users find it harder to move between platforms. Open XR interfaces and standards may therefore become a less visible but very important part of progress.

Network technology will shape social VR as well. Shared presence requires synchronization of avatar positions, voice, objects, and events. Latency that is tolerable when loading a web page becomes obvious in live conversation or coordinated action. The future of virtual worlds therefore depends not only on the headset, but on the infrastructure around it.

Artificial intelligence may change content creation by accelerating modeling, animation, character behavior, and adaptation of environments. It also creates new questions about authorship, errors, and moderation. The more autonomous a virtual character becomes, the more important it is to know what it can do, where its data come from, and how its behavior is constrained.

Working in VR does not necessarily mean spending an eight-hour day inside a closed headset. A more likely pattern is a series of specialized episodes: reviewing a 3D model, collaborative design, training, a remote meeting, and then a return to other interfaces. Everyday use may consist of short, useful modes rather than permanent immersion.

Cultural acceptance cannot be derived from device specifications. Cameras in public places, avatars in work meetings, digital clothing, and virtual property will acquire social norms gradually. What is technically possible may be socially awkward, then become ordinary, or remain niche.

The final forecast of this course is deliberately modest. VR will almost certainly continue to develop as a family of spatial interfaces and simulations. The form of mass adoption remains open. Knowing the subject well does not mean claiming the future is already known. It means being able to distinguish durable technical trends, real evidence of benefit, and the next beautiful presentation.

The future of virtual reality also depends on which tasks become valuable enough that people are willing to put on a device. A few hours a week may be acceptable for gaming. Work places much stricter demands on weight, text clarity, battery life, and social comfort. One headset does not have to solve every scenario equally well.

The market may continue to support several classes of devices: specialized headsets for professional tasks, consumer systems for games and communication, and mixed-reality devices in which the digital layer does not always hide the physical world. This is not a prediction about specific brands, but a consequence of different requirements for different uses.

That diversity of scenarios keeps the final question open. VR may change the world not as one single "new reality," but as a set of tools that gradually enter medicine, education, design, entertainment, and communication. A technology's influence often becomes larger than its original label.

One possible direction involves distributing computation between the device and external systems. Local processing reduces latency and can help privacy, while cloud resources can handle heavier tasks. The balance depends on networking, energy use, and the demands of the particular application.

Another direction is more natural input. Hands, gaze, and voice reduce dependence on controllers, but they do not eliminate conventions. For precise work, a physical button may still be better than a gesture. Future interfaces are likely to be multi-modal, using different forms of input for different tasks.

Photorealistic avatars are improving too, but their success depends on more than appearance. Facial expression, gaze, voice, and body movement all have to arrive at the right time. The more realistic the face becomes, the more noticeable even a slight mismatch is.

New devices will inevitably create new privacy norms. Persistent cameras, room maps, and gaze tracking require rules that were unnecessary for an ordinary monitor. Technological development is therefore always accompanied by institutional development: laws, standards, and social norms.

The final conclusion of the course can be stated simply. VR influences the world when it gives people a new way to see, act, and learn in space. Its value is not determined by the number of digital worlds. It is determined by how precisely the technology solves a human problem and how responsibly it treats the person inside it.

PORTRAIT: IVAN SUTHERLAND AND MORTON HEILIG: TWO UNFINISHED FUTURES

Heilig imagined a medium that addressed several senses at once. Sutherland wrote about an "ultimate display" capable of creating convincing perceptual objects. Their devices have long since become obsolete, but the questions remain. The history of VR is a reminder that the future rarely realizes an old dream literally. It breaks the dream into engineering problems and assembles it again.

PLOT TWIST: THE MOST SUCCESSFUL VR MAY STOP BEING CALLED VR

If spatial interfaces become ordinary, users may stop treating them as a separate technology. Sometimes a label disappears not because a technology failed, but because it dissolved into everyday life.

KEY TERMS

Spatial computing – an approach in which digital objects and interfaces are organized in relation to physical or virtual space.

Haptics – technologies that provide tactile feedback.

Brain-computer interface (BCI) – a system that uses measurable brain signals to communicate with or control a device.

Metaverse – a loose term for persistent, interconnected digital spaces and services.

Interoperability – the ability of systems to exchange data or work together.

Photorealism – visual quality that approaches a physically plausible scene.

Spatial interface – an interface placed and controlled in three-dimensional space.

TEST

Choose one correct answer.

1. Why may the future of VR blend with AR and MR?

a) Devices increasingly combine virtual and physical layers

b) VR will stop using displays

c) AR requires closed eyes

d) MR does not use cameras

2. What matters for a mass-market device besides graphics?

a) Only polygon count

b) Weight, heat, battery life, and comfort

c) Brand name

d) Box size

3. Why does touch remain a difficult problem?

a) Skin cannot feel

b) Vibration is the same as weight

c) Touch has no connection to the brain

d) The system has to act physically on the body, not merely display a signal

4. What is true of current BCIs?

a) They can already read any thought

b) They do not exist

c) They work with limited measurable signals and are not complete mind-reading systems

d) They are only for games

. . .

5. Why should the term "metaverse" be used carefully?

a) It refers to different concepts without one single implementation

b) It is one mandatory protocol

c) It refers only to cinema

d) It means any 3D file

6. What can happen to a successful VR technology?

a) It must remain a separate headset

b) It may dissolve into everyday interfaces

c) It will stop using computation

d) It will become only a game

7. What technical challenge ran through the whole course?

a) Increasing advertising

b) Making all scenes identical

c) Eliminating head movement

d) Keeping system signals aligned with human perception and action

8. How should predictions about the future of VR be treated?

a) Believe the most spectacular one

b) Reject every prediction

c) Separate demonstrated technology, prototype, and promise

d) Treat advertising as a scientific paper

9. What matters most in a useful simulation?

a) Fit with the task and a measurable outcome

b) Maximum photorealism in every case

c) The longest possible session

d) The most expensive device

10. What is the main skill this course should leave you with?

a) Memorizing every headset model

b) Memorizing advertisements

c) Asking precise questions about a technology, its capabilities, and its consequences

d) Learning to use one specific engine

HOME EXPERIMENT

- Finish your "My Virtual World" project. On one page, bring together its purpose, user, space, locomotion method, three interactions, avatar, measurable benefit, privacy rules, and one technological limitation you will not hide. End with one sentence: why should this project exist in VR rather than on an ordinary screen? If you cannot give a convincing answer, that is also a useful design result.
- *The main course is complete. The remaining sections bring together answers to every test, a general glossary, resources, and recommendations for further reading and viewing.*

AFTERWORD

At the beginning of the course, virtual reality looked almost like a trick. Two images, lenses, sound, and a handful of sensors can make a person treat a digital space as a place. We have now taken that trick apart. We know that presence does not live in any single component. It emerges when vision, movement, sound, and the system's response are coordinated well enough.

The history of VR also turned out not to be the story of a single inventor. The stereoscope learned to give the two eyes different images, the panorama filled the field of view, simulators showed the value of safe simulation, computer graphics provided a scene that could change, and sensors linked that scene to the movement of the head. Modern VR emerged when these lines of development could finally work together quickly enough and cheaply enough.

Then we discovered that a technical victory is not the same as a human one. You can build a beautiful scene and make the user nauseous. You can give the user hands and make the gesture unclear. You can create a realistic avatar and destroy the sense of naturalness with one wrong facial movement. VR keeps reminding the designer that the final system includes the human body and perception. It does not end at the display.

That is why the most interesting uses of VR appear where the properties of the technology actually match the task. A spatial simulator is useful when an action must be repeated safely. Virtual exposure can form part of therapy when a frightening situation needs to be presented in a controlled way. An engineer benefits when scale and ergonomics must be judged before anything is built. An educational scene earns its place when it helps someone understand space or practise an action, rather than merely making an impression.

The same logic applies to risk. A headset does not "steal thoughts," but it does measure movement, and some devices collect data about gaze, hands, the face, and the surrounding room. The more tightly a computing system is coupled to the body, the more important data minimization, local processing, clear permissions, and boundaries of behavior in social spaces become.

The future of VR therefore cannot be reduced to a single forecast. Separate, enclosed virtual worlds may remain important for games, training, and some professional tasks. Much of the technology may instead dissolve into mixed reality and spatial computing. Haptics, comfortable optics, battery life, and social acceptability may prove no less important than increases in graphics power.

After twelve evenings, it is useful to keep one way of testing any new claim about VR. Ask: what signal does the person receive, what does the system measure, how quickly does it respond, what result is being promised, how was that result tested, and what data must be given up in return? These questions separate working technology from an impressive demonstration.

Virtual reality is interesting precisely because it sits on a boundary. It is digital, yet it acts through the body. It can be fictional, yet provoke real responses. It lets us build a world that does not exist and then use it to test very real skills, decisions, and rules of behavior. We have learned to step inside an image. The main question is no longer whether that is possible, but what is worth building there.

ANSWERS TO THE TESTS

The explanations are deliberately brief. Their purpose is to return you to the logic of the answer, not to replace the lesson. If an answer surprises you, reread the relevant part of the chapter.

LESSON 1

1. b – The system changes the scene in response to the user's movements.

2. a – The experience of being located in a virtual environment.

3. c – The technical conditions of immersion.

4. d – It adds digital elements to the physical world.

5. b – Visual information triggers a real protective response.

6. d – The system responds to the user's actions.

7. a – XR.

8. c – The environment must respond coherently to the user's actions.

9. d – The user changes the viewpoint through movement.

10. b – To simulate difficult and dangerous situations safely.

LESSON 2

1. b – A separate image for each eye.

2. d – Wide visual coverage.

3. a – It used several sensory channels.

4. b – He linked the computer-generated image to the position of the head.

5. c – Because of its great weight.

6. d – The technology grew out of many different fields.

7. a – Several essential components were still immature at the same time.

8. b – Displays, computing, and tracking had matured.

9. c – An idea can wait for the right components to become available.

10. d – How the eyes derive depth from two images.

LESSON 3

1. d – To reproduce the slightly different viewpoints of the two eyes.

2. b – A change in the apparent position of objects as the observer moves.

3. a – To make a nearby display usable by the eyes and create a field of view.

4. c – Field of view.

5. d – The brain uses several cues to depth.

6. b – It computes the image of the scene.

7. a – A change in the focusing of the eye.

8. c – The inward turning of the eyes when looking at a nearby object.

9. d – Changes must remain consistent as the head moves.

10. b – Focal distance does not change as it does in the real world.

LESSON 4

1. a – Three translations and three rotations.

2. c – Rotational motion.

3. d – To compensate for the weaknesses of different data sources.

4. b – The headset estimates its position using its own cameras.

5. a – They change shape and occlude one another.

6. c – Latency.

7. d – The image must quickly match the movement of the head.

8. b – It measures acceleration.

9. a – It does not fully track position in space.

10. c – An accurate and rapid link between movement and scene updates.

LESSON 5

1. c – A group of unpleasant symptoms that can occur in VR.

2. d – Conflicting signals from different senses.

3. a – Vision indicates movement without corresponding movement of the body.

4. b – To reduce continuous visual motion.

5. c – Turning by physically stepping.

6. d – No.

7. a – Stop or change the session.

8. b – The content and the method of locomotion.

9. c – Poor design can cause physical symptoms.

10. a – To building a scene under limited computing resources.

LESSON 6

1. b – From a polygon mesh.

2. c – How a surface behaves under lighting.

3. d – The scene must be drawn quickly for two eyes while the head is moving.

4. a – It defines the region used for collision detection.

5. b – The computer calculates behavior according to rules.

6. c – It helps localize sound sources.

7. d – An environment for assembling interactive scenes.

8. a – Blender.

9. b – A sensible distribution of detail.

10. c – A drop in frame rate.

LESSON 7

1. d – The relationship between the user's actions and the system's responses.

2. a – Familiar physical cues may be missing.

3. b – Physical buttons and precise input.

4. c – People look at things without intending to select them.

5. d – To show that an action has been registered.

6. a – Controller vibration.

7. b – There is no fixed screen frame, and viewing distance changes.

8. c – Through light, sound, and movement.

9. d – A cue that suggests a possible action.

10. a – To the question of the virtual body and avatar.

LESSON 8

1. a – A digital representation of the user.

2. c – The feeling that a body or body part belongs to you.

3. d – The feeling that you are the author of your own action.

4. b – The sense of body ownership depends on integrating sensory signals.

5. a – It links visible movement to the user's action.

6. c – The feeling that other people in a virtual environment are present nearby and available for interaction.

7. d – It records movement so that it can be transferred to a digital model.

8. b – Errors in facial expression and movement become more noticeable.

9. a – Personal-space boundaries and movement data.

10. c – It participates in bodily and social perception.

LESSON 9

1. b – It allows a situation to be repeated without paying the full cost of a mistake.

2. d – Skill transfer or another measurable outcome.

3. a – For controlled exposure.

4. c – The ability to assess space at human scale.

5. b – The parameters of a complex environment can be controlled.

6. d – Applying what was learned in another situation.

7. a – Computer-aided design.

8. c – What outcome was measured.

9. b – A simulation can isolate the skill that matters.

10. d – Results cannot automatically be generalized to every real-world situation.

LESSON 10

1. a – Working with spatial objects and objects that are difficult to access.

2. b – A strong impression may not lead to understanding.

3. d – The mental resources demanded by the task.

4. a – Part of the learner's attention is spent on operating the system.

5. c – When space or action is part of what must be learned.

6. a – Applying knowledge in a new situation.

7. b – To compare the effect of an intervention.

8. d – Testing whether knowledge is retained and can be applied.

9. c – It reduces distracting load.

10. b – To the question of data, influence, and responsibility.

LESSON 11

1. d – Head movement.

2. c – It reveals the direction and duration of attention.

3. a – The surrounding physical space.

4. b – Processing on the device itself.

5. d – They control a substantial part of the user's sensory environment.

6. c – Manipulative choice architecture.

7. a – Virtual proximity can provoke a real psychological response.

8. b – Whether a flow of data is appropriate depends on context and norms.

9. d – No. It depends on the data and the method.

10. c – What happens if VR becomes an ordinary computing environment.

LESSON 12

1. a – Devices increasingly combine virtual and physical layers.

2. b – Weight, heat, battery life, and comfort.

3. d – The system must physically affect the body, not merely display a signal.

4. c – They decode limited, measurable neural signals for specific tasks; they do not provide unrestricted access to a person's thoughts.

5. a – The term is used for different concepts without a single implementation.

6. b – It may dissolve into everyday interfaces.

7. d – To align the system's signals with human perception and action.

8. c – Distinguish what has been demonstrated from a prototype and from a promise.

9. a – A good fit with the task and a measurable outcome.

10. c – The ability to ask precise questions about a technology, its capabilities, and its consequences.

GENERAL GLOSSARY

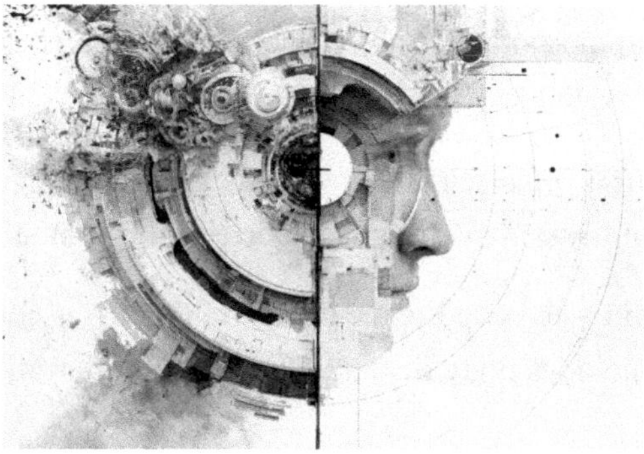

3DoF – three degrees of freedom, usually rotations only, without full tracking of movement through space.

6DoF – six degrees of freedom: three translations and three rotations tracked for the head or controller.

Accommodation – a change in the optical power of the eye's lens that allows objects at different distances to be brought into focus.

AR (augmented reality) – digital elements are overlaid on the visible physical world.

Avatar – a digital representation of a user in a virtual environment.

BCI (brain-computer interface) – a system that records measurable neural signals and translates selected features of those signals into commands, communication, or other output.

Body ownership – the feeling that a body or body part belongs to you.

CAD – computer-aided design: the use of computers to design objects and systems.

Cybersickness – nausea, dizziness, disorientation, eye strain, and other unpleasant symptoms experienced by some VR users.

Embodiment – the experience of a virtual body as connected to oneself; it includes body ownership, agency, and spatial self-location.

Eye tracking – measurement of gaze direction and, depending on the system, other aspects of eye movement.

FOV (field of view) – the portion of space visible through a display system.

FPS – frames per second; one measure of how frequently the image is updated.

Haptics – technologies for tactile feedback, such as vibration, pressure, or resistance.

HMD – head-mounted display, a display or headset worn on the head.

Immersion – a system's technical capacity to surround the user with coherent sensory and interactive signals.

Inside-out tracking – tracking the position of the headset and controllers using sensors and cameras on the headset itself.

Interactivity – a system's ability to change its state and scene in response to the user's actions.

Latency – the delay between an event, such as head movement, and the corresponding response from the system.

Motion capture – recording the movement of a person or object so that it can be transferred to a digital model.

MR (mixed reality) – an environment in which digital and physical elements coexist and can be spatially related.

OpenXR – an open API standard that defines an interface between XR applications and XR runtime systems across different hardware platforms.

Outside-in tracking – tracking in which external cameras or base stations observe the headset or controllers.

Presence – the experience of being in a virtual environment as a place where events are happening around the user.

Rendering – computing the image of a virtual scene from a specified viewpoint.

Room-scale VR – a VR mode in which the user physically moves within a tracked area.

Social presence – the feeling that other participants in a virtual environment are nearby and available for interaction.

Spatial audio – sound designed to convey the direction and sometimes the distance of a virtual source.

Teleportation – a method of locomotion in VR in which the user selects a destination and is moved there without continuous visual travel along the route.

Vergence – the coordinated turning of the eyes required to fixate on an object at a particular depth.

Vergence-accommodation conflict – a mismatch between the vergence cue and the display's focal distance, common in many current VR systems.

VR (virtual reality) – an interactive digital environment that uses a display, tracking, and other channels to create the experience of being inside a scene.

WebXR – a web API framework that lets compatible browsers present VR and AR experiences on supported XR hardware.

XR – an umbrella term for VR, AR, MR, and related technologies that connect physical and digital environments.

Avatar – see the Avatar entry above.

Agency – the feeling that your intention caused the action of a virtual body or object.

Accelerometer – a sensor that measures acceleration.

Vestibular system – the inner-ear system and related neural structures involved in sensing acceleration, rotation, and head position.

Gyroscope – a sensor used to measure rotational motion.

Engine – a software environment that brings together rendering, scene management, physics, input, sound, and other components of an interactive application.

Cognitive load – the amount of mental resources required to perform a task at a given moment.

Collider – a simplified geometric region used by a physics engine to determine collisions.

Convergence – the inward turning of the eyes when looking at a nearby object; a particular case of vergence.

Local processing – processing data directly on the device rather than necessarily sending it to a remote server.

Material – a set of parameters that determines how a surface looks and interacts with light.

Metaverse – not a single technical standard, but a group of concepts involving persistent, connected virtual spaces and digital identity.

Optical flow – the pattern of visible image motion produced by movement of the observer or the scene.

Motion parallax – the change in the relative positions of objects in the visual field as the observer moves.

Polygon mesh – a 3D form built from vertices, edges, and faces.

Spatial mapping – building a digital representation of the geometry of the physical environment.

Predictive rendering – computing an image using the predicted position of the head at the moment the frame will be displayed, in order to reduce perceived latency.

Sensory conflict – a mismatch between what different senses report about movement and the position of the body.

Stereoscopy – creating a sense of depth by showing different images to the left and right eyes.

Texture – an image or set of maps used to define the color and fine surface properties of a 3D object.

Tracking – measuring the position, orientation, or movement of the head, hands, eyes, or other objects.

Dark pattern – an interface technique that steers the user toward a choice that benefits the system through manipulative design.

Foveated rendering – a method that allocates rendering quality according to gaze direction, devoting more resources to the region of central vision.

Exposure therapy – a psychotherapeutic approach in which a person gradually and controllably encounters feared stimuli; VR can be used to deliver that exposure.

Novelty effect – a change in attention or motivation caused by the unfamiliarity of a technology, which may not persist once the user becomes accustomed to it.

RESOURCES

The sources below support the factual and conceptual parts of the course. For rapidly changing technical standards, official project pages or specifications are listed; their current versions should be checked before a new edition of the book.

LESSON 1

Slater, Mel; Wilbur, Sylvia. "A Framework for Immersive Virtual Environments (FIVE): Speculations on the Role of Presence in Virtual Environments." Presence, 6(6), 1997, pp. 603–616.

Slater, Mel. "Place Illusion and Plausibility Can Lead to Realistic Behaviour in Immersive Virtual Environments." Philosophical Transactions of the Royal Society B, 364, 2009, pp. 3549–3557.

LESSON 2

Wheatstone, Charles. “Contributions to the Physiology of Vision. Part the First. On Some Remarkable, and Hitherto Unobserved, Phenomena of Binocular Vision.” Philosophical Transactions of the Royal Society, 1838.

Sutherland, Ivan E. “A Head-Mounted Three Dimensional Display.” Proceedings of the Fall Joint Computer Conference, 1968, pp. 757–764.

Computer History Museum. Collection materials on Ivan Sutherland and early head-mounted display research.

LESSON 3

Howard, Ian P.; Rogers, Brian J. Perceiving in Depth. Oxford University Press, 2012.

Hoffman, David M. et al. “Vergence-accommodation conflicts hinder visual performance and cause visual fatigue.” Journal of Vision, 8(3), 2008.

LESSON 4

Khronos Group. OpenXR 1.1 Specification, current revision. Sections on spaces, poses, and input.

MDN Web Docs. WebXR Device API and Fundamentals of WebXR. Documentation on pose tracking and rendering loops.

LESSON 5

Kennedy, Robert S. et al. "Simulator Sickness Questionnaire: An Enhanced Method for Quantifying Simulator Sickness." International Journal of Aviation Psychology, 3(3), 1993.

Simón-Vicente, L. et al. "Cybersickness. A systematic literature review of adverse effects related to virtual reality." Neurología (English Edition), 39(8), 2024, pp. 701–709.

LESSON 6

Akenine-Möller, Tomas; Haines, Eric; Hoffman, Naty. Real-Time Rendering. 4th ed., CRC Press, 2018.

Khronos Group. glTF and OpenXR documentation for real-time 3D asset and XR pipelines.

LESSON 7

Jerald, Jason. The VR Book: Human-Centered Design for Virtual Reality. ACM Books / Morgan & Claypool, 2015.

Norman, Don. The Design of Everyday Things. Revised and Expanded Edition. Basic Books, 2013.

LESSON 8

Botvinick, Matthew; Cohen, Jonathan. "Rubber hands 'feel' touch that eyes see." Nature, 391, 1998, p. 756.

Kilteni, Konstantina; Groten, Raphaela; Slater, Mel. "The Sense of Embodiment in Virtual Reality." Presence, 21(4), 2012, pp. 373–387.

LESSON 9

Freitas, José Rúben Silva et al. "Virtual Reality Exposure Treatment in Phobias: a Systematic Review." Psychiatric Quarterly, 92(4), 2021, pp. 1685–1710.

Morina, Nexhmedin et al. "Can virtual reality exposure therapy gains be generalized to real-life? A meta-analysis of studies applying behavioral assessments." Behaviour Research and Therapy, 2015.

LESSON 10

Radianti, Jaziar et al. "A systematic review of immersive virtual reality applications for higher education: Design elements, lessons learned, and research agenda." Computers & Education, 147, 2020, Article 103778.

Makransky, Guido; Petersen, Gustav B. "The Cognitive Affective Model of Immersive Learning (CAMIL)." Educational Psychology Review, 2021.

LESSON 11

Nissenbaum, Helen. Privacy in Context: Technology, Policy, and the Integrity of Social Life. Stanford University Press, 2010.

Miller, Mark Roman et al. "Personal identifiability of user

tracking data during observation of 360-degree VR video." Scientific Reports, 10, 2020, Article 17404.

Nair, Vivek et al. "Unique Identification of 50,000+ Virtual Reality Users from Head & Hand Motion Data." 32nd USENIX Security Symposium, 2023, pp. 895–910.

Khronos Group. OpenXR 1.1 Specification, current revision, especially the sections on runtime capabilities, spaces, input, and permissions. Platform privacy rules remain implementation-specific.

LESSON 12

Khronos Group. OpenXR 1.1 Specification, current revision. A useful reference for cross-device XR application and runtime interfaces.

MDN Web Docs. WebXR Device API. The current browser-facing API model for virtual and augmented reality on the web.

Silva, Alexander B. et al. "The speech neuroprosthesis." Nature Reviews Neuroscience, 25, 2024, pp. 473–492. A current review of what neural decoding can achieve in a specific clinical domain, and of the limits that remain.

WHAT TO READ AND WATCH NEXT

Jason Jerald. The VR Book: Human-Centered Design for Virtual Reality. If the course leaves you wanting to understand how VR can be designed around human perception and behavior, this is one of the most coherent routes through the engineering and design questions.

Tomas Akenine-Möller, Eric Haines, Naty Hoffman. Real-Time Rendering. A book for the next technical level. It goes far beyond this course and shows what happens between a 3D scene and the finished frame.

Mel Slater and Sylvia Wilbur. A Framework for Immersive Virtual Environments. A classic paper that is useful because it carefully separates properties of the system from the experience of presence. It is a good example of how scientific terminology can make a debate more precise.

Ivan Sutherland. A Head-Mounted Three Dimensional Display. A short historical primary source from 1968. It is worth seeing how recognizable the basic ideas of a modern HMD already were in work written long before today's consumer devices.

Khronos OpenXR. Not a textbook, but a living technical specification. Useful if you want to understand how a modern application communicates with different XR devices through a shared model of spaces, poses, and input.

MDN WebXR. A practical entry point into browser-based XR. Best for readers who already know some web development and want to see what tracking and rendering look like at API level.

Research on embodiment: Botvinick & Cohen; Kilteni, Groten & Slater. These works show why the virtual body is not a decorative part of the interface, but a tool for investigating the sense of one's own body.

Systematic reviews of VR therapy and cybersickness. The best way to avoid the trap of a single impressive demonstration. Reviews show where findings repeat, where studies differ, and what limitations remain.

WELCOME TO THEHAPPYSTORYGARDEN!

Dear reader, if you have found this book either useful, interesting or simply enjoyable, please leave feedback. We appreciate it very much. Thank you. TheHappyStoryGarden.com

www.ingramcontent.com/pod-product-compliance
Lightning Source LLC
LaVergne TN
LVHW050815061126
851857LV00012B/808
* 9 7 8 1 8 0 6 9 7 0 9 6 4 *